CW01637657

HOW TO CARE FOR YOUR PASTOR:

A guide for small churches

HOW TO CARE FOR YOUR PASTOR

A guide for small churches

KENT PHILPOTT

EVP Earthen Vessel Publishing

EP EVANGELICAL PRESS

EVANGELICAL PRESS

EVP

Evangelical Press
Faverdale North, Darlington
DL3 0PH England
Evangelical Press USA
P.O. Box 825, Webster NY 14580 USA
email: sales@evangelicalpress.org
www.evangelicalpress.org

Earthen Vessel Publishing
289 Miller Avenue,
Mill Valley, CA 94941 USA
www.earthenvessel.net

Co-published by Evangelical Press and Earthen Vessel Publishing
First published 2008

British Library Cataloguing in Publication Data available
ISBN 978 085234 6662

PRINTED AND BOUND IN THE USA

Dedicated to the people God has placed in the church to lead his flock, those who have been appointed to the single most important responsibility that can be given to any person

contents

preface

IN 2000, I wrote *For pastors of small churches*. It focused on the small church. Since so much attention has been given the large church, I thought something was needed for the small church. After all, most churches are small. This book is a companion piece to that book for pastors.

My empathy for pastors has grown considerably since the publication of *For pastors of small churches*. Over these past seven years, I have received dozens of emails, letters, phone calls and personal visits from pastors scattered all over the world. As a result, I began to question the very institution of the pastoral ministry. I have wondered if we have not missed our way and wandered instead into an unbiblical model of church organization that is hazardous to the health and well-being of pastors and their people alike. I am aware I am only one of probably thousands of Christians who have struggled with and questioned the dominant paradigm we have inherited for congregational life. However, no one I know has come up with an acceptable alternative that passes biblical muster for the gathered saints in worshipping and serving the Lord our God, so I will settle for working on and tinkering with what has been handed down. I bring no revolutionary thinking then, but I do intend to be as plain as I can without crossing ordinary boundaries of decorum. I mean, *I want to tell it like it is.*

One reviewer thought that readers might think I was somewhat unbalanced and that I should have been working with a psychotherapist before attempting to write about pastors and congregations. Perhaps so much revelation about the inner life of a pastor in such a condensed manner is the reason for the reviewer's perspective. In thinking how I might change the manuscript to meet such concerns, I was afraid that I might sanitize the actual life of the pastoral ministry and thus forfeit my hope that church congregations would appreciate and understand the real life of a pastor. If a congregation is to care for a pastor, it is necessary for that congregation to know who and what a pastor is — in real time and in real life. In fact, it may occasionally seem as though I am writing with pastors in mind as readers and not congregations. Again, my goal is to communicate something of how pastors think and feel, so that congregations may be able to think and feel along with them. It is difficult to care for pastors without knowing something about their lives.

Recently I read a book about Tony La Russa, manager of the St Louis Cardinals, and what I enjoyed most of all was learning something of how a big-league baseball manager thought — those inner details that are not revealed in a box score. I am hoping to do a little of the same by revealing what being a pastor has been like for me personally.

Another reviewer pointed out that there was a great deal of *me* in the book, making it too autobiographical. It is possible to use stories of pastors I know for illustrations, but I need to maintain confidentiality. Therefore, I primarily rely on my own pastoral experiences.

On 2 October 2006, I celebrated the fortieth anniversary of my ordination. The Excelsior Baptist Church in Byron, California, ordained me, and Robert D. Lewis, then pastor of the First Baptist Church of Fairfield, California, preached the ordination sermon that very hot day in Byron. He was the pastor who first preached the gospel to me, baptized me, confirmed my call to the ministry and sent me off to Golden Gate Baptist Theological Seminary in Mill Valley, California. My dad was there, as were my wife and children, but my mother refused to attend. The Excelsior faithful were present plus some visitors from the community. My pastorate at Byron lasted two-and-a-half years. Then I was involved in the Jesus Movement from 1967 to 1972 and functioned, for much of the time, as a leader of a para-church ministry. As an outgrowth of that ministry, I began pastoring a church in San Rafael, California, an independent charismatic congregation. It was not a small church, but neither was it a large church — averaging about 300 people on Sunday mornings. During my years in San Rafael, the church planted a number of other churches, and I served as an overseer to some of those churches. In September 1984, I began pastoring a small congregation of elderly people, which became Miller Avenue Baptist Church of Mill Valley, California, on 1 July 1985. I am still at Miller Avenue.

I provide this background information so it can be seen that I have some experience as a pastor. Clearly, I am still learning how to do the work, but I care very much for pastors, and therefore, I present this small volume.

My retirement from the pastoral ministry is rapidly approaching. My twin daughters will graduate from high school in June 2008, and then it might be time for me to relocate and begin another phase of ministry. The day I leave Miller Avenue will likely be the saddest day of my life since I love this congregation so much. Old time gospel preachers like me never actually retire, but it seems to me that pastoring a small church like Miller Avenue requires a younger man. But the idea of my leaving started me thinking about a little book I had written in the 1970s, a book written for congregations on how to care for their pastors. I had not attempted to have it published, and I was not sure I still had a copy of the manuscript; a search through my archives uncovered it. Maggie Bates and Mary Bischoff from the Miller Avenue congregation typed it out anew and created a Word document of it. I merely had the pleasure of going back over that thirty-year-old manuscript, reworking and updating the material. I was shocked at how that youngish pastor understood the need for congregations to care for their pastors.

And this is my concern: for churches to know how to care for their pastors. The content of this book is more applicable to the smaller church since pastors of smaller churches are usually more personally involved with the congregation. Of course, what is presented here about pastors and churches will be applicable to any size church.

The subject matter of three chapters — 'The pastor is vulnerable', 'The pastor may become spiritually bankrupt' and 'The pastor must be free to fail' — will seem to overlap. This is intentional, and the overlapping is real. Rather than have one long chapter, I decided to separate the chapters from each other so that the nuances that distinguish the three chapters might be more readily apparent.

Several people have helped with editing the manuscript: Katie Coddaire, Pam Joaquin and Tom Jerrells. Janice Van Eck did the final polishing. Thank you dear friends.

Scripture references are taken from the English Standard Version (ESV). For those who have decided preferences about versions of the Bible, my view is that there is no perfect translation, especially since we do not have the autograph copies, but the ESV 'works for me' as they say.

Each chapter begins with an anecdote, conversation or other 'teaser' that relates to the chapter's subject. Then there is the body of the chapter, concluding with some questions for congregations.

Suggestions, comments and critiques are welcome. Please email them to kentphilpott@comast.net or post them to Kent Philpott, 289 Miller Avenue, Mill Valley, CA 94941, USA.

Readers might be interested in other books I have written. These are:

- *Are you really born again?* Now in an expanded second edition, it speaks to the issue of true and false conversion.
- *Why I am a Christian.* This book consists of a series of essays originally written for *Evangelical Times*, a Christian newspaper published by Evangelical Press, headed by a lead article titled, 'Why I am a Christian'. It is primarily for non-Christians.
- *Are you being duped?* is an edgy and contemporary apologetic focusing on key issues in an evangelistic manner, excellent for non-Christians.
- *For pastors of small churches* is of course about pastoring the small church — fifty-seven chapters of practical issues.

Kent Philpott
Mill Valley, California
1 January 2008

introduction

WHAT ARE the problems, pressures and needs of those who pastor the people of God? How can the fellowship of believers encourage and minister to these key members of the church family? The aim of this book is to provide some answers for these questions.

Christians care about their ministers, elders, shepherds, priests and pastors — whatever the title may be — for it is they who bear the burden of leadership. (For simplicity sake, I will use 'pastor', as it seems to be the most common description.) These pastors are the Moseses, the Joshuas, the Davids and the Timothys, the men God has called to speak his Word, bring guidance to the faithful, comfort the bereaved and afflicted, work with the rebellious and encourage the hopeless. What, though, can the saints do to *hold up the arms* of those whom God has placed over them in spiritual authority?

First, the leaders can be appreciated for who they are. Ministers are often seen as superstars, perfected saints, demagogues, dictators, deluded persons, eccentrics, 'holier-than-thou' types and stuffed shirts. Such caricatures are usually errant and never helpful. Second, the problems peculiar to church ministry can be understood in relation to the minister. It is my guess that many of the saints don't realize the challenges their leaders experience. The real life of the pastor is often hidden, either intentionally or unintentionally, from the congregation. And third, believers can come to a fuller understanding of their relationship to God's appointed authorities in the body. The shepherd is a sheep too, but has been made a shepherd of sheep; nevertheless, he is still one of the sheep.

There will never be a perfect pastor. And there will not need to be as long as we know there cannot be. Jesus, who is himself the Head of the Body, is the only perfect one. Our Minister is perfect, wholly trustworthy and faithful, the King who will never fall off the throne.

> Now may the God of peace who brought again from the dead our Lord Jesus, the great shepherd of the sheep, by the blood of the eternal covenant, equip you with everything good that you may do his will, working in us that which is pleasing in his sight, through Jesus Christ, to whom be glory for ever and ever. Amen (Hebrews 13:20-21).

one

The pastoral ministry: preaching the gospel, teaching the Word

'I understand you are a priest, or reverend, or pastor — I'm not sure which is the right term. I always wondered what people like you do.'

'Pastor is the word I use for myself, and mostly I work an hour a week, Sunday morning you know, then I take it easy the rest of the week playing golf, fishing, attending meetings — that kind of thing.'

'Really?'

'No, not really. What I actually do is preach the good news of Jesus to non-Christians and teach the Bible and its doctrines to Christians.

It is a full-time job, and I love it.'

WHAT DOES a pastor do? There are a number of answers. The above dialogue, though made up for this chapter, does express how some people view the pastoral ministry. And whenever I am asked to describe who I am and what I do, I tend to respond in much the way I expressed above. Preaching and teaching, this is what I do, and I need my church to support this work, for if they don't I will not be able to do it.

Someone might state, 'The primary responsibility of a pastor is to love the congregation.' I agree. My loving of the congregation means that I want each person to be genuinely converted and to grow up into the fulness of Christ. Therefore, I preach the gospel and teach the Word. This is *agape* love, and it is the seeking of the highest good for each person. That great good is being in fellowship with the Maker of heaven and earth. All sentiments, feelings and brotherly or sisterly love pale into insignificance compared to the love of God in Christ Jesus.

This is chapter one; it was not in the original version I wrote in the 1970s. I now know that the preaching and teaching of Jesus is the single most important job of a pastor that must be supported and encouraged by his church.

A key passage

'And they devoted themselves to the apostles' teaching and fellowship, to the breaking of bread and the prayers.'

Acts 2:42 is a key passage because it states the priorities of the early church, that church very close in time to Pentecost and before gradual, inevitable corruption entered into the churches.

'Apostles' teaching' is first in the list. The content of that teaching would be what Jesus both said and did — essentially what we find in the four Gospels. We also find aspects of the apostles' teaching in the other letters and books of the New Testament, those written by Luke, Paul, Peter, John, James and Jude, as they applied what they learned from and about Jesus and communicated it to the early church, both Jewish and Gentile.

Jesus told his followers to make disciples of others, to baptize them and to teach them all that they themselves had been commanded (Matthew 28:19-20). The last thing Jesus told his disciples was: 'But you will receive power when the Holy Spirit has come upon you, and you will be my witnesses in Jerusalem and in all Judea and Samaria, and to the end of the earth' (Acts 1:8). There was one last opportunity to speak face to face, and Jesus gave his disciples what was foremost on his mind: *they must be his witnesses.* This is at the top of the list, the great priority in the job description of every pastor — everything else is secondary.

Paul made clear the great importance of the Christian witness when he said, 'So faith comes from hearing, and hearing through the word of Christ' (Romans 10:17). The outcome of that faith is everlasting life, but there must be a hearing of the word of Christ — thus the need for the preacher. Indeed, everyone who calls upon the name of the Lord will be saved. God elects, calls and saves, but not without the agency of the preacher.

> But how are they to call on him in whom they have not believed? And how are they to believe in him of whom they have never heard? And how are they to hear without someone preaching? And how are they to preach unless they are sent? As it is written, 'How beautiful are the feet of those who preach the good news!' (Romans 10:14-15)

The pastor is a preacher and a teacher. First comes preaching and then teaching — a simple model for the work of the pastor/preacher/teacher.

Preachers and teachers: God's gifts to the church

In Ephesians 4:11 Paul lists gifts given to the church by Jesus Christ: 'And he gave the apostles, the prophets, the evangelists, the pastors and teachers.' Notice that 'pastors' is joined to 'teachers' by 'and', which is a coordinating conjunction in the Greek and leads to the idea the two are closely linked together. It may be concluded that the pastor is also a teacher.

All Christians are preachers in the sense that all Christians are to bear witness to Jesus and the gospel. However, pastors do much of the preaching. To the Corinthian Church, Paul explained how very important the work of preaching is. After describing the dramatic change that takes place when a person becomes a Christian and becomes a 'new creation', Paul wrote:

> All this is from God, who through Christ reconciled us to himself and gave us the ministry of reconciliation; that is, in Christ God was reconciling the world to himself, not counting their trespasses against them, and entrusting to us the message of reconciliation. Therefore, we are ambassadors for Christ, God making his appeal through us (2 Corinthians 5:18-20).

How clear the importance of teaching and preaching is! Pastors, above all else, need to be supported in the preaching of the gospel of Christ and in the teaching of the Apostles' doctrine. The Scripture makes a huge point of it. Paul instructed Timothy: 'Let the elders who rule well be considered worthy of double honour, especially those who labour in preaching and teaching' (1 Timothy 5:17).

The 'elders' — possibility a synonym used for pastors by the early church — did preach and teach, and, for that reason, they were to be accorded double honour. What 'double honour' means is not perfectly clear, but to say these preachers and teachers were to be supported and encouraged in that work is not missing the mark.

Pastors need help

Why would pastors need to be encouraged in the work of preaching and teaching? Over the years, I have formed some opinions about this, being a gospel preacher and Bible teacher myself.

One, the unconverted do not like hearing that they cannot save themselves, since they are dead in their trespasses and sins (Ephesians 2:1) What non-Christians like to hear is that there is something they can do to make themselves acceptable to God.

Prior to my conversion I didn't like hearing that I was hopelessly lost and unable to do a thing about it. I would have preferred being given something I could do like joining the church or being baptized or helping others, anything to do other than turning from sin and trusting that the blood of Jesus was powerful to cleanse me of my sin. Rebel that I was, like we all are, the story of salvation did not sit well. I took it out on the preacher, too. I thought he was a dumb hick from Arkansas and delighted in saying so to members of his congregation. He was from Arkansas, but he was a courageous, bright and committed preacher of the gospel. And he kept it up until I was converted. Thank you, Lord!

Criticism from those who hate the gospel may be intimidating or taken personally by pastors. The reactions of those who are under conviction of sin can have a chilling effect. To counter this, congregations can encourage their preachers to continue with the gospel.

Two, not all members of churches respond warmly to being taught what it means to be a committed follower of Jesus. 'If anyone would come after me, let him deny himself and take up his cross and follow me' (Matthew 16:24). How Christians struggle with this! We bring *baggage* of various sorts into our new life in Christ, and leaving that baggage behind can be a painful process.

Three, there is an enemy who delights in dragging people into hell with him, and he is angry with pastors who preach a clear and strong gospel. The devil will tolerate gospel light that has a works salvation motif running through it. A doctrine of grace and good works combined is no threat to the dark side. In fact, the devil will encourage that sort of preaching. Many are attracted to the dumbing down of the biblical gospel.

Four, those who think they are converted but are not — people in the congregation itself who may have considerable influence in the affairs of the congregation — may attempt to move a pastor into preaching that which will not 'offend'. This is often masked as preaching meant to attract new congregants or to ease up on existing congregants — people who obviously have heard enough evangelistic messages. However, my experience tells me that born-again Christians love to and need to hear the gospel preached, and preached in many ways and from many texts. About three out of four of my sermons have a clear gospel message, even when I am preaching doctrine to *the choir* as it were. I think of the young C. H. Spurgeon who wandered into a Methodist chapel when the pastor could not make it due to a snowstorm, but nevertheless, he heard a gospel message and was converted. If something similar were to happen at Miller Avenue, I want the message of the gospel to be heard. I am not always preaching for conversions, but the central story of the person and work of Jesus will appear, and prominently, in most every sermon. Nothing is so interesting for the Christian as the gospel, and we do testify that we love to hear the story of Jesus and his love.

Five, troubles in the church family, the pastor's family, troubles with money, the local community, health problems and so on, serve to wear preachers and teachers down. Congregations may be able to help in these times. I am convinced it takes more physical energy and spiritual strength to proclaim the Word and the gospel than any other topic. No research data exist on this, as it would be largely unmeasurable, still this is my sense of it.

Six, pastors will take public stands on moral issues such as homosexuality and political corruption, and will thereby earn the disrespect of those who take offense. This has happened to me on numerous occasions. Presently, our Miller Avenue Baptist Church is sponsoring an outreach to those who struggle with homosexual temptation and want to be Christians. This effort has come to the attention of the local media, and a number of pieces have appeared in local papers attacking us; of course, much of this is aimed directly at me. Some pastors are courageous enough to stand up for truth and justice but still cannot do it alone without strength and encouragement from the congregation.

Congregations can be aware that their pastors experience these troubles and may find means to help bear some of the burden. It is often enough for people to understand the pressures that may descend on the pastor. For me, this often makes the difference, just to know others know, care and are praying with me. In Psalm 23, David did not say that God delivered him from his dark and dangerous valley, but that God *walked with him* through it. I count on it that not only does God walk with me, even carry me at times, but my brothers and sisters in Christ are with me as well.

Ideas on how to encourage pastors

A simple 'thank you' goes a long way in encouraging pastors. Flattery is not called for, but a word of thanks is appreciated. Even when I have preached what I thought was a poor sermon, people have pointed out something in the message that helped them — and I was encouraged.

Attentiveness is a big boost. There are several people at Miller Avenue I watch while I preach or teach. They look me in the eye; they even lean forward during the sermon and will have their Bible open with a pen in hand. Paying attention, being keen to learn and grow — this may be the very best way to encourage a preacher or teacher. Asking questions on a subject, if the format allows, is a definite stimulant. Questions that are well thought out, not off the top of one's head, and questions not meant to trap or upstage a teacher but honest, real requests for clarification will keep a teacher motivated to prepare well and understand that his labour is not in vain.

Doing what you say you will do is a way to encourage church leaders. Yes, I have impulsively volunteered and not followed through; we all have done this. In the church, however, the impact of failing to keep our commitments can be significant. I would rather have someone decline a request, even taking time for consideration, than say yes and not act on his or her good intentions.

A pastor's confidence can be eroded in the face of continual disappointments.

Being on time, with bright eyes and a smile on your face, indicates a readiness to hear and absorb. A thumbs up or a pat on the back is good, too. Bringing others to hear the preaching and teaching is very uplifting.

A congregation can make sure the preacher and teacher have good study tools. Usually this is not necessary, but it may be needed. An English dictionary, Bible dictionary, exhaustive concordance, interlinear Greek-English New Testament and interlinear Hebrew-English Old Testament are valuable. My favourite single-volume commentary on the whole Bible is the *International Bible Commentary*, general editor F. F. Bruce. I have several sets of commentaries and many commentaries on individual Bible books. My favourite book on preaching is by D. Martyn Lloyd-Jones, *Preaching and Preachers*. Lloyd-Jones' book is so encouraging to me that I attempt to read it through every year. C. H. Spurgeon's *Lectures to my Students* is both inspiring and informative.

Preachers and teachers need time to study, and this may have to be secured by the congregation. Often the morning hours, before lunch, are the best and many wise congregations protect their preachers and teachers from interruptions and other appointments during this time. Perhaps the best reason why pastors are paid a salary is so they can study and prepare. Good sermons and Bible studies don't just happen! Be patient with preachers and teachers — it takes years to develop solid preaching and teaching skills. I commonly tell young pastors that it will take ten years of regular preaching to reach the stage of a beginner. This may seem like an exaggeration, but I think not. It seems to me, and to some who have known me for forty years, that I am only now preaching my best sermons.

Ideas on how to discourage pastors (a short list)

Words are powerful; once spoken they cannot be retracted. Here is a list of questions and comments that I am not fond of hearing and that can *discourage* a pastor with even the stoutest of hearts.

- 'How come there are so few of us?'
- 'Where is everybody?'
- 'What are we doing wrong?'
- 'Where is the blessing of God?'
- 'How come we are not growing?'
- 'That new church sure has exciting programs.'
- 'I wish we had a preacher like that new church has.'
- 'How come the Smiths left the church?'
- 'I wish we could do things differently around here.'
- 'We get too much Bible preaching here.'
- 'We don't get enough Bible preaching here.'

A concluding thought

A favourite text at ordinations is 2 Timothy 4:1-5, where Paul, writing one last time to Timothy, his beloved partner in the work of the ministry, speaks about the great work of a pastor. As you read it once again, see how directly it speaks to the subject of this chapter.

> I charge you in the presence of God and of Christ Jesus, who is to judge the living and the dead, and by his appearing and his kingdom: preach the word; be ready in season and out of season; reprove, rebuke, and exhort, with complete patience and teaching. For the time is coming when people will not endure sound teaching, but having itching ears they will accumulate for themselves teachers to suit their own passions, and will turn away from listening to the truth and wander off into myths. As for you, always be sober-minded, endure suffering, do the work of an evangelist, fulfill your ministry.

Pastors have faults and inadequacies. To have men who will preach the gospel and teach the Word, you must encourage and support them.

For further thought . . .

1. What do you want most in a pastor/teacher?
2. Have you ever known a *perfect* pastor?
3. What would giving 'double honour' to a preacher/teacher look like?

two

The pastor is a person

While I was counselling with a young couple, the wife complained about certain behaviours of her husband. All the while he squirmed in his chair and looked miserable. As I listened, it occurred to me that in some respects I was quite like the young man, and eventually I broke in and said so.

Tinged with some annoyance, her immediate response was, 'I don't believe it. *You're a minister.*'

MANY PEOPLE in our churches do not understand that the pastor is a person, someone not unlike everyone else. In the eyes of the young woman above, I wasn't a person. I was some kind of little god or perfected saint — someone different, better, unlike the young man she married.

All the common frailties

A pastor is a person and, therefore, has the usual frailties common to the fallen human race. This is no excuse for bad behaviour on the part of a pastor but it is an important acknowledgement that a pastor is a human being. Yes, there is a higher standard that a leader in the church is called to, a trust that is to be honoured, but the pastor is still a person who is growing up into the stature of the fulness of Christ. 'Sanctification' is what theologians call this growing up. It is a process that takes all our lives and is never complete this side of being face to face with God in heaven, when we will be no longer looking through a glass darkly.

Jesus as a person

Christians are sometimes amazed at some of the descriptions of Jesus they stumble upon in the Gospels. The four evangelists show him as being weary, hungry, thirsty, sorrowful and angry. It can be difficult to accept Jesus as a man when we know that he is God, albeit the God-man. The church leader, though not God in any sense, can also be weary, hungry, thirsty and much more — mad, hateful, frustrated and unloving. In fact, pastors are vulnerable to any sin imaginable. It can accurately be stated that every minister, priest, pastor, indeed every leader in Christ's church, is a sinner.

Peter, that great patriarch of the church, was a man and a sinner. After the great confession, 'You are the Christ', came the denials. He became a pillar in the church at Jerusalem, but Paul rebuked him for compromising the gospel of grace. What are we to think of Peter the great apostle? He was a sinner just like every other person who has ever been called into the Kingdom of God, neither inerrant nor infallible.

A moment of shame

I was surprised to find that a minister from another city had made an appointment with me. His name was familiar, and I didn't think too highly of the church he pastored. Of course, he didn't know what I thought. But he wanted to talk to me, and due to the fact that we were not close, I guessed whatever it was he wanted to talk about must be of some importance to him.

As the appointed hour grew near, the more expectant and excited I became. Was I going to find that this pastor was having trouble with his church? It was as though I was about to experience a personal triumph. Compassion, love, prayerfulness — none of these entered my heart or mind. When I recall the incident, I am still embarrassed about my reaction.

'How are you doing?' was my opening line. This pastor, who was older than me just nodded. He sat down and stared at the floor. His red eyes told me he'd been crying. Guilt feelings surged through me and every ounce of my one-upmanship drained away. As far as I remember, I've not shed a tear since I was twelve, but I almost did then. The story he related is by now one I am used to hearing. His church had become a great burden. Attendance was way down, as were the offerings. People were grumbling; he was straining and striving, and ready to give up on himself. And he had come to me, a fellow brother in Christ who was glad of the thought of gaining something over him. After he talked, I talked. Softly and haltingly I told him how I'd felt about the appointment and asked him to forgive me. It was hard to do, and I probably would have hid it from him had he not been in such a pitiable state.

Here were two pastors, two sinners, who felt nothing like perfected saints. I wasn't even feeling 'Christian', nor had I acted like one, until God changed my attitude. Is this usual? No! Can Christian leaders really act this way? Yes! Why? Because they are human beings.

Feet of clay

A pastor lives life as anyone else, facing the process of aging, physical illness, marital problems, troubles with the kids, misunderstandings with the neighbours, cars breaking down, being overweight, being uncertain about the future and so on. Time and life invariably expose the limits of our strength and ability and will without fail reveal that our feet are made of clay.

A few pastors I have known chose to distance themselves from the people they served. Yes, there is something to be said for being aloof and inaccessible. It is possible, though not very authentic, to hide behind titles, vestments and false impressions. Some of us simply have a difficult time being known as the human beings we are. We want to transcend our limitations and at least pretend to be more than we are. We want to be liked, approved and esteemed. Perhaps it is the pastors ourselves or the aura of the office, handed down through the centuries, that creates the distance between pastor and congregation and indirectly contributes to an exaggerated sense of the pastoral ministry. If people think pastors are more than human, maybe pastors are partly at fault.

Some pastors who have come to realize that they are being suffocated trying to live the perfect life act out in various ways, intending to prove to everyone that they are just human beings like the rest of the congregation. I have known some rather awkward efforts by church leaders to accomplish this. Some took up smoking, drinking and other even more dangerous behaviours — all to convince or warn others that they were just regular people. (This would call for exceptional caring for congregations.) Most often passing quickly but embarrassingly, such conduct will sometimes convincingly prove that pastors have feet of clay, or something even less honourable.

The *clay* metaphor as applied to ministers of the gospel comes from 2 Corinthians 4:7: 'But we have this treasure (the gospel of the glory of Christ) in jars of clay, to show that the surpassing power belongs to God and not to us.' Pastors are jars of clay; they need to know it, and their congregations need to know it as well or the glory will be misplaced, credited to people rather than to our glorious Christ. Proper appreciation of this means better health for both pastor and congregation.

God does not need superstars; he wants real people who are

committed and obedient to him. Being who we are allows God to make us who he wants us to be. Because of who God is and the love he pours out on us, we can be who we are and allow those who minister to us to be who they are.

In summary

Part of caring for pastors involves coming to grips with their humanity, their fallen nature, their struggles to grow up into Christ, and their failures and limitations. This certainly is how church members want their pastor to relate to them. Remember that wonderful golden rule: do to others as you would have done to you. Of course, this does not mean accepting, excusing or tolerating bad behaviour or, as it is sometimes expressed, it does not turn the congregation into co-dependents. It also does not mean shunning, rejecting and disrespecting a pastor when things are not going well or even are going terribly.

God is a miracle-working God, a God who can bring glory out of the worst situation, and God is not a God who gives up on people, even pastors. Pastors may need to be pastored from time to time, without their knowing it maybe, by mature brothers who know what it is to be human, a saint and a sinner all at once.

For further thought...

1. How do you view pastors? Are they different?
2. Do you recall a time when a pastor cared for you?
3. What meant most about that ministry to you?
4. Can you pastor a pastor?

three

The pastor is growing

'Kent, when do you think you will have your emotions under control? I saw you become upset this morning with that question during the Bible study? I am looking for a church that has a pastor who is more assured and in control of his emotions. Sorry, I hope you don't mind if I keep looking for another church.'

I understood. It had been my hope that by the time I was forty I would be a mature person. Then I thought maybe fifty, then sixty. Now I have given it up. There has been growth, but I have a long way to go.

WHEN PASTORS are ordained, they are fully equipped to minister the gospel of Jesus Christ. True or false?

Why isn't the answer 'true'? It is not true because a pastor is growing and changing.

Change is to be expected

Looking back on my life I see I have changed. This is clear to us when we think about our past and compare how we were with how we are. It is probable, however, that we are not fully aware of all the ways in which we do grow. At the least, we grow emotionally, theologically, psychologically, spiritually and physically. It is essential that Christians understand that *pastors* are growing and changing too. Growth means change, and some changes can surprise us.

Pastors grow emotionally

Ministers grow emotionally. Everyone deals with insecurity and fear, for example. Being one-of-a-kind in a large or even small society can produce painful situations. Over-sensitivity has always been a problem of mine. Probably due to feelings of insecurity, when I am criticized or confronted about my sermons, it can have an impact me. As the years pass, however, the criticisms, negative comments or helpful suggestions have helped me to become a better preacher. Actually, I *need* the feedback, but I have to be emotionally strong to *benefit* from it.

One Sunday I preached a sermon on the basics of the second coming of Christ. Later that day I received a phone call from someone who had heard it. I was told that it wasn't adequate because I'd presented only one side. Admittedly, eschatology is not one of my strong points, yet the criticism hurt. Over the course of the next few months, I had opportunity to read several books on the subject. What my critic had said proved to be true. I had, in fact, presented only a part of the picture. Now I seek to give as balanced an understanding of Christ's second coming as possible. Though I was hurt at first, I benefitted from the correction.

Parenthood is a job you are only somewhat capable of doing by the time the children are grown and gone. A father or mother doesn't necessarily know how to be one, and a husband or wife always has a long way to go. Yet, in the Bible we see that a pastor has to be a good father and husband or he shouldn't be in spiritual leadership. There is a large guilt trap hidden somewhere in there. Church leaders are learning to cope with a myriad of complicated and never-ending family responsibilities, and churches can expect that their pastors will make the same mistakes they do — maybe more.

For me, there seems to be a direct relationship between my ability to minister in the church and my ability as a father and husband. The question is, How much more growing is yet ahead for me? At this point, there is no way of knowing, but I still have a lot of growing to do.

Pastors grow theologically

Theological education, discipleship, leadership training, seminars and conferences are all wonderful, but they cannot teach church leaders all they need to know about the Bible, Christian doctrine and how to lead a congregation.

Years ago at a Christian festival I heard 'Holy' Hubert Lindsay of Berkeley speak. That man could recite the whole Bible; he had it memorized from Genesis to Revelation. As I listened to him, I was at once impressed and depressed. Obviously impressed, but discouraged by the fact that I had, at that time, only a few dozen passages committed to memory. I was just learning the Bible. I know more of the Scripture now than I did thirty-five years ago, and I hope to know yet more.

Some of what I learned in the church where I was converted I have dropped or altered. Doctrines I embraced during my seminary years I no longer accept. There were doctrines I stood by rigidly only to find that I am more open now to nuances and differences. Some things I am completely unsure about and rarely even speak of anymore. Do you suppose this is unusual in a preacher?

Over the years, I have not become liberal. If anything, I have become more biblical and Christ-centred than ever before. I refer to myself as an 'old time gospel preacher'. My great pleasure is to preach Jesus and teach the Word. But I have changed theologically over the years. It has been a great blessing that my dear Miller Avenue Church has given me room to do this without condemning or challenging me. Without fear, I can speak openly about biblical doctrines I am examining. Understand that I am not talking about the major doctrines that we see outlined in the Apostles' Creed, the doctrines that make Christianity distinct from all the world's religions. Pastors, however, like anyone else, will interact with the many and various trends that come along, some of which involve and impact biblical theology. Early in my ministry I embraced trendy doctrines without question only to be burned when they fizzled and faded. Each time a movement passed through, I had to examine the theology that went with it — and my theological perspectives would grow and change. This process continues to this very day, but such changes can be unsettling to churches and can even erode the confidence congregations have in their pastors.

There may be changes in theology

Church leaders' theology will change. It must, since the Bible is hugely complex and Christian doctrine is so deep and wonderful that it would take many lifetimes to make a significant dent in understanding either one.

Sometimes my theology was shaky, especially during the Jesus Movement, when I was faced with charismatic expressions of Christianity after having earlier been immersed in dispensational theology. I can count four distinct eras of my doctrinal life — the usual for many American evangelicals — because I tended to follow the trends.

The second coming of Christ is a good example of my theological wanderings. I have embraced several models. I was probably right at some point — I just don't know for sure when! Also, I have moved from an Arminian theology, where human will triumphed over God's will, to a Reformed viewpoint. For twenty-nine years I was a solid believer in the power of human decision-making; now I see God alone has that prerogative. I changed, and it shocked the congregation. Instead of throwing me out or fighting me every time it could be seen that I was changing views, they supported me. They did not necessarily embrace my new directions, but they struggled with me as I worked through what I had to work through.

Miller Avenue is a rather curious group with some even holding to more Calvinistic theology than myself, some less so, and some amused at my Puritanisms, all the while remaining Arminian in theology themselves. It is indeed a spiritual, theological diversity, and I think this is healthy.

I have known pastors who have changed in some point of theology and have had to resign as a result. Their congregations were not mature enough to work through a very natural and necessary experience or did not have the personal and spiritual security to allow the pastors to work out their salvation with fear and trembling. I have known pastors who stumbled badly over certain central doctrines but went on to make corrections along solid biblical lines. In each case, the church would have lost an excellent pastor if the congregation had had a rash reaction.

Pastors grow psychologically

It can be conveyed to seminary graduates, either explicitly or implicitly, that they are something special. A congregation desperately looking for a pastor may send a similar message, and it is quite disappointing for pastors to find that instead of being special, they are common. Congregations may be confident that time will whittle away at the preachers and teachers psychologically to make them the people they need to be. People of God, be warned and be sympathetic — your spiritual leader's sense of self or ego may undergo change.

Having a strong sense of personal worth and security is not easily achieved by anyone, and a pastor must have a considerable amount of both. We remember that the devil is the accuser of our brothers (Revelation 12:10), and the accusations tend to damage our sense of self, stripping us of personal confidence. There have been times when I could barely stand before the congregation because my confidence had been so shaken. Gospel preaching requires spiritual and psychological courage, and a pastor beaten down by the 'accuser' may be rendered ineffective. Congregations need to support their ministers with their prayers and practical encouragements, a kind of lifting up of the arms of Moses.

Pastors grow spiritually

After my conversion I read a pamphlet about spiritual disciplines. In it was an account of the devotional life of Billy Graham, a Christian I have always admired. Every day the great evangelist read two chapters of the Old Testament, along with three Psalms and a chapter of Proverbs, then two chapters from the New Testament. Then he would pray; I believe he used a prayer list, too. I copied Billy Graham and held to his system faithfully for many years. As time went on, I developed my own method. Along with Bible reading and prayer, I added a time of worship. For several years during the 1970s, I would spend entire afternoons in worship and prayer. I find I spend much more time in study and preparation for sermons now, and far more time reading good Christian literature.

There have been dry periods with little or no prayer and much less Bible reading. Other times I have had an enormous hunger after God, as if I was freshly in love with God again.

The nature of my spirituality has certainly changed, and I think I am more confident in my walk with the Lord than ever before. To an outsider, however, it might not appear that way.

Personal reflections

When I was a little boy, God was very big and way, way up there. Now that I am a man, God is still very big and way up there, but through Jesus and the ministry of the Holy Spirit, I have a personal relationship with him, which is still developing and growing. Since *God* does not change, it must be that *I* am changing. I've learned that I cannot hide this from the congregation, nor do I want to. Some of my best sermons are embedded in my growing up into Christ and allowing this dramatic and visible sermon to be observed. Pastors see their church members grow up in Christ and the church will see their pastors grow up in Christ as well.

Another biblically-based metaphor, that of running a race, is appropriate. I am running a race: I started well, stumbled a time or two, but have kept my eye on the goal, the upward call of God in Christ. In the grandstands are fans who encourage me, and with the encouragement given to me, I am enabled to encourage others in their races. I hope by his grace to finish the race strongly, with my last days, and especially my dying days, being among my best observable sermons.

Pastors grow physically

I am now sixty-five years old. Some of what I was able to do years ago I can no longer do. Some of what I used to be able to do I still do, but I don't do it quite as well. Best of all though, some things that I did poorly I now excel at. My preaching is stronger, according to some of the church family who have heard me for nearly two decades. My teaching is stronger, because I know more of the Scripture now than ever before. Like a good old piece of hickory wood, I am seasoned, tough and useful.

There may come a time when I will not be able to preach and teach as much or as often as I do now. Those days will come. Miller Avenue is a small church, and I do many tasks, happily and willingly, but I know some of these side jobs will have to be done by others.

Dear friends at Miller Avenue know changes must come and have already begun to talk about how to share the work and spread it out amongst the fellowship, in order to allow me to remain at my primary work. There is talk of my preaching until I am eighty; there are those pastors who do, and even longer. Whether I die in the pulpit or not, I am comforted that the congregation recognizes my aging and have some plans in mind.

Giving the resources to grow

Churches that understand that their leaders are constantly developing emotionally, theologically, psychologically and physically are more likely to provide the freedom and resources to do so.

Pastors love conferences where peers gather for fellowship and teaching. Some of my most significant growth, vertical and horizontal, has come as a result of such *ministers'* meetings. Churches can see to it that their pastors are able to attend these from time to time. Then there are books, magazines and journals, which require money. Pastors may be reluctant to express their need for books. Maybe the church could arrange a sabbatical to attend classes, even earn another degree — the church will benefit too. Helping to find a mentor, perhaps an older, experienced pastor, can also be valuable. And vacations — vacations are important, and not merely a weekend once in awhile.

If a congregation accepts and understands that pastors change and grow and allows for these processes to take place, the whole experience can be a great blessing to both pastor and congregation.

For further thought...

1. How well do you know your pastor?
2. What do you expect of your pastor?
3. Jesus' theology was mature and complete. Was Peter's?
4. When might a church leader come to have a theologically finished product?
5. What steps might a church take to ease the work of an aging pastor?

four

The pastor is not a saviour

'Pastor, you can't retire. You've given so much and we have a wonderful ministry here. Everyone would be terribly disappointed.'

'I do appreciate how you feel and I know my last day at Miller Avenue will be the saddest day of my life. All my friends are here, and I consider this church to be my extended family. But it must come, and you will get along without me, though it will be a big loss for all of us.'

THAT THE PASTOR is not a saviour is abundantly clear from the last two chapters, not to mention the obvious teaching of Scripture. Why then would a chapter with such an emphasis be needed?

The human condition

It seems to be part of the human condition to look to another person for emotional and spiritual support. Infants are totally dependent on their parents for sustenance. To small children, though they are not as dependent as infants, the parents are still vital. It is during later childhood that we find our heroes.

Adolescence is a time for acquiring heroes, but then begins the emancipation process that leads the teenager into young adulthood. This period can be a time of rebellion, especially when parents are found to be less than perfect and childhood heroes fall away.

Teenagers need not rebel in a dangerous way, but a distance, a separation from parents will develop, must develop, in the life of a healthy young person. Distance and separation from parents is a good thing and makes a future adult-to-adult relationship possible. I prefer to call it a partnership, like that which I currently have with my three adult children.

Young adults will strike out on their own, distanced from parents to some degree, and find their adult identity. Most often these young people resemble the parents in many ways, but they will also be different. Then comes the next generation and the whole process starts all over again. This is family life. This is also congregational life.

Pastors as heroes and saviours

Human development is mirrored by the spiritual. At age twenty-one, the age I was born again, I began to develop spiritually. At first, I entered into the infantile stage where I could digest only the milk of the Word (1 Peter 2:2). I was spoonfed as it were; I was given spiritual milk to drink. It was as though God was cradling me in his arms, protecting me from any hurt. During the Sunday morning services, as I bowed my head in prayer, in my mind's eye I could see the pastor brilliantly silhouetted against a black background. He was special. Before my conversion, I had thought he was an ignorant, prejudiced man. How quickly my opinion changed! Jesus was becoming increasingly real to me, but he didn't stand up to preach each Sunday, nor did he stand at the back door to shake my hand and speak a personal word to me. There was the pastor, and I sensed he liked me. Later, I was asked to teach Sunday school, which brought me into closer contact with my pastor. He eventually asked me to do a special ministry at a juvenile hall. I was growing up into preadolescence. That pastor, Robert D. Lewis, who is yet living and my friend, had an influence in my life that he knew nothing of.

A day of growing up

First Baptist Church of Fairfield, California, had a team in a church softball league. I either played left field or sat on the bench. The pastor was the shortstop and played the game well. He was the most intense man on the field, especially when we played one particular team, the Mormons.

It was in the late innings one very hot Tuesday night in August. It was hot in many ways. I can recall that moment with extreme clarity. Pastor Lewis hit a line drive between the left and centre fielders, 'in the gap' it is called, and was going for a double. Their second baseman, in taking the throw from the left fielder and attempting to make the tag, spiked the sliding preacher. And he was out.

My hero of the faith jumped up and chased that second baseman through the infield then out into centre field with players from both teams running after them. I sat in shocked silence. Here was my pastor, screaming after this guy. I grew up that night right into adolescence.

Actually, I didn't outright rebel, but I saw something I needed to see. The man who had baptized me was not the saviour. I still loved and respected the man, but there was an empty place inside of me, nevertheless. I had yet to develop into a partnership in the ministry with him — but I would.

Growing separation

After that incident, I listened more critically to his sermons, and I started forming my own conclusions about what the Bible taught. No longer did I automatically believe every doctrine I heard preached. In a sense, I'd been pushed out of the nest. Once out and on my own, I borrowed heavily from what my pastor had taught me, though I did not become a carbon copy or facsimile; rather, I found myself working in the ministry of the gospel just like my old pastor. Though not in close proximity, we were partners in the ministry.

Some people have been through the same process with me. No, it is not that I had to fall off the pedestal, but they experienced spiritual growth and could stand with Jesus on their own.

At times, it hurt me to see this. The closeness that had been there was gone; the spiritual parent-child relationship had been altered. There have been those who had considerable trouble making the adjustment. Rather than transition, it was rebellion. Strangely, the most rebellious have been those with whom I'd spent the most time, those into whom I'd poured a lot of myself. Some rebelled to the point they joined 'better churches'. Perhaps it would not have happened if I had been aware of the spiritual growth process and in turn had taught it to the congregation. I don't want anyone to look to me as a saviour, but there are those who, in the beginning of their Christian lives, will do just that.

Pastors cannot be saviours

Pastors cannot be saviours since they need one themselves. Every pastor sings along with, 'It's me, it's me, O Lord, standing in the need of prayer.' I know better than anyone else in my church that I am a sinner saved by grace alone. With Paul I cry, 'Wretched man that I am!' Though I am not, though I do not want to be, for a period of time in some newborn Christian's life, I will seem to be a saviour. When that Christian matures, I hope he or she will accept me for who I am: a simple person called to minister for Christ in his Body, the church.

Who is that pastor anyhow?

If a pastor is not a saviour, who is that ordained person anyway? A pastor is a person God has placed in a position of spiritual authority in the church. The pastor as a feeder of the sheep cannot feed unless the sheep are willing to be fed. Pastors pastor when they are allowed to pastor. The church must recognize and submit to the authority of its ministers, recognizing all the while that pastors are just ordinary people whom God has placed over them. The authority of Christ actually rests, not ultimately or perfectly, in those he has appointed as apostles, prophets, evangelists, pastors and teachers. Even with such a glorious appointment, they will err.

My primary responsibility is to communicate Jesus Christ in his fulness to the rest of the fellowship. This does present a problem. Since I am not a saviour, since I have a limited understanding of the Bible, how can I possibly bear adequate witness to the greatness of Christ? The answer is quite simple: I can't. However, I am to be faithful to preach and teach the gospel of Christ and trust in the Holy Spirit to do the inward regenerating and renewing work. The living and written Word is not all perfectly revealed to me, and it will never be this side of heaven. To me this means that at times I will do well and at other times I will not do well. I can be comfortable with that now that I know I'm not a saviour and, especially, when my congregation knows that as well. Hopefully, as I seek to faithfully preach Christ as Saviour and worship him, those for whom God has made me spiritually responsible will also see that I am not a saviour.

For further thought ...

1. Do you have a pastor who is a hero to you?
2. Have you had a pastor who has fallen off the pedestal?
3. Do you recognize the stage of spiritual growth you are presently in?
4. Can you see your relationship with your pastor as a partnership?

five

The pastor needs the respect and support of the congregation

Several years ago, the pastor of a nearby church wanted to talk with me. He picked me up in front of our church building, and we drove downtown to a coffee shop. Being about the same age and with similar pastoral experience, he and I had developed a friendship over the years.

He showed me a copy of a letter that had been sent out to his membership by a disgruntled elder. As a Lutheran pastor, he faithfully preached law and grace, but this one elder wanted more grace and less law. My friend was upset and did not know exactly how to deal with the problem. He would continue to preach in the time-honoured and traditional ways of Lutheranism, that much was clear. Now though, he could sense the unease in the congregation.

A year later, he was gone. The congregation found a pastor who would preach what it wanted to hear. As congregational support and respect began to wane, a climate was created that my friend was not able to weather.

THOUGH A PASTOR is growing up into Christ, and certainly not the saviour, every pastor needs the respect and support of the members of the congregation. It is as though churches give permission to their pastors to pastor, preach and teach.

Judging pastors

My first and only pastor warned against having 'roast preacher' for Sunday dinner. We in the congregation laughed each time he said this, not thinking he was serious. But he was; I lived to know exactly what he meant.

Pastors live openly, almost in the proverbial fishbowl. Their words and actions are public. They preach the perfect law of love and are obviously not perfect. Therefore, respect and support may not come easily. Then too, pastors often do things people do not understand.

In my second pastorate, where I served as senior pastor, we attempted to practise discipline according to Matthew 18:15-20. The very first time we had to follow through on a disciplinary action it resulted in two people being asked to leave the church. It was a time of prolific and malicious gossiping, whereby the church leadership was accused of a multitude of relatively minor wrong-doings. On examination, our board of pastors accepted some blame and worked to make corrections. The flow of criticisms directed at the elders though made our work difficult. As a young and relatively inexperienced pastor, I saw first hand how a loss of support and respect could impact a congregation.

The couple in question returned some time later with an apology and a request for forgiveness. The process took nearly a year, and several church members left in protest and never returned. If, however, proper respect and support had been shown for the leaders, perhaps greater glory would have been given to Christ. That event, over thirty years ago now, taught me an important lesson: God calls us to give honour and respect to our leaders no matter what the institution — government agency, sports organization, church and so on. Respecting the work of leaders is a direct way of giving support, even though we do not fully understand or appreciate their every action.

Lessons from my first pastorate

I began my first pastorate at twenty-four years of age. The median age for the congregation was around forty. These people had worked hard to keep their small rural church alive — then I showed up from the seminary. For six months I served as an interim pastor, then they called me as pastor and tried to treat me as such. I struggled to gain their respect and support. Most of them knew more of the Bible than I did, and the vast majority were far more emotionally and spiritually mature than I was.

I admit I was forever pressuring that small congregation into new ministries. There was a migrant worker's camp close by, and I would spend a considerable amount of time with the workers and their families. Also, in our area was a juvenile lock-up facility for boys, which I visited regularly. The result was an almost full chapel each Sunday and a series of baptisms. One year, our small church nearly led our association in baptisms. Yet, each Sunday became a painful experience for all of us, however full the pews were. The regular members would remain after the teenage boys and migrant workers moved on, which they knew would happen when I left them — as seminarians usually did after graduation. Therefore, they would not support the new forms of outreach.

Towards the end, I was becoming anxious on Saturday nights. I no longer looked forward to the work. Without the support of the congregation, I did not have what it took to continue. I resigned.

I couldn't earn my congregation's respect and support, and they wouldn't or couldn't give it. Instead, we struggled with each other, though in a very Christian way. Looking back at it now, I feel that if they had been able to stand with me, I might have turned from my somewhat skewed vision for outreach so that we could have moved ahead together.

Respect and support is not unconditional

I will repeat the central premise of this chapter: pastors simply cannot minister unless they have the respect and support of their congregation. I am not speaking of blind trust or absolute obedience, which may be seen in destructive cults. Where leaders break the law or where people are being abused or treated unjustly — this leadership is to be spurned and rejected. Nor am I suggesting churches overlook ministerial sin just to keep the boat from rocking. But short of major crimes and misdemeanors, any unbiblical theologies and methodologies, inexperience and personality clashes — or experimenting with new ministries — should not precipitate a withdrawal of support and respect.

The new pastor

Respect and support must be given at first and then earned thereafter. When a congregation receives a new pastor, respect and support must be given without it having been earned, obviously, since no track record has been established. No pastor will conduct a ministry that will please everyone. Wise pastors will study a church and observe what has been working. Some forms or emphases will be retained, but others will be discarded and new ones will be put in place. This is where trouble often begins — the discontinuance of certain established ministries and the founding of entirely new programs. Here is where the congregation needs to be supportive and encouraging. If a particular ministry fails, it should fail on its own and not because it has been sabotaged.

Each pastor will have certain gifts and feel confident doing some things and not others. A comfort level will be discovered, mostly through trial and error. Whether a person is new to a church or new to ministry as such, there must be some experimenting. Nothing is automatic about gospel ministry. God's purposes and ways do not always look the same from place to place or person to person. *Flexibility* is a key word. A congregation is best served if it is flexible and adaptable and allows leaders room to operate.

I have begun a number of ministries that ultimately failed. Some folded quickly; others died slowly. This I can accept, but when members of the congregation deliberately set out to be obstacles, my leadership is undermined. If there are a string of such events, fruitful ministry is almost impossible to achieve.

Double honour

Paul, who had considerable experience with pastors and churches, said, 'Let the elders who rule well be considered worthy of double honour, especially those who labour in preaching and teaching' (1 Timothy 5:17). Notice the rule well part. (By *rule*, I think Paul meant lead.) There will be pastors who do not rule or lead well. Those who do not necessarily lead well and/or are not as charismatic in personality, yet lead, are still to be considered worthy of honour. All the ministers who labour in ministry, however talented, are to be respected and esteemed.

It must be asked: How would it be known whether pastoral leadership was sound or less than that? How, especially in the short run, can a judgement be made? Doing new things or doing old things differently is not the criteria. Usually new ministry needs time to develop and evolve appropriately. In my career, I have seen ministries flounder for lengthy periods only to finally break through and have some success. Others went through nearly complete metamorphosis and proved vital. Spur of the moment decisions can be costly in many ways.

Paul has something else to say that bears on our topic: 'But we ask you, brothers, to respect those who labour among you and are over you in the Lord and admonish you, and to esteem them very highly in love because of their work' (1 Thessalonians 5:12-13). Paul asks that double honour be given elders who lead or rule well, especially for those who preach and teach. In this passage, he says to esteem them very highly in love — for the sake of their work. I know that without the love and support of the congregation I work in vain.

How we begin is not always how we finish

Honouring leaders will help them grow, because it provides an atmosphere that fosters growth. As a young pastor, I did not know what I was doing; I was not fully mature emotionally or physically and hadn't even graduated from seminary. After ten years of seminary and several degrees, I still had little idea of what I was doing. Of course, I had some idea, but from my perspective now, I was barely adequate. At least I know now that I am essentially a preacher of the gospel to non-Christians and a teacher of the Word to Christians. But I did not start this way.

I also know now that I have been carried along by the inner working of God's Spirit, and I think that has come to me mostly through the people in my congregation. These dear people are not fans cheering from the stands; fans can boo as well as cheer. No, these are people I work alongside of to do the work of the gospel. We are partners labouring in the fields, and we give mutual support and encouragement. Members of the church family have stood by me over the years and inspired me to carry on.

A better way

There are one or two ways in which I can minister to a person who confesses a sin to me. I can contribute to their feeling miserable and worthless or I can help them turn from their sin and then seek to build up and encourage them. Of course, I aim for the latter. A congregation can actually stir their pastor up to good works by showing respect and support. My people love me, and I love them. From my viewpoint, they loved me first. Their loyalty challenged me to a greater loyalty to Christ as well as a greater loyalty to my job as their shepherd. When I preach or teach in my fellowship, I do it with confidence and boldness because I know that my brothers and sisters are for me, even urging me on. It's a liberating experience. I don't fear their judgement or condemnation. And they don't have to 'amen' me either; I know where their hearts are.

Respect and support in real time

What does respect and support of a pastor look like in the life of a church? Though far from exhaustive or complete, here are some practical ideas.

Handshakes, smiles, nods and attentiveness surely help. Showing up, being on time, being faithful with supporting the work, praying for, thanking, refusing to gossip, sending a note of appreciation — these are important because they communicate support and encouragement. Sticking with a leader through difficult times, in times of disagreement and conflict, says that leader is still appreciated.

We can be assured that the church that experiences the fulness of what God has for them is a church that respects, supports and loves their *busy* pastors.

For further thought ...

1. Have you experienced respect and support in your life?
2. Have you experienced the opposite?
3. How important is it to you that those with whom you live and work both respect and support you?
4. How might you react in the absence of respect and support?
5. In what tangible ways can a church demonstrate respect and support for their pastor?

six

The pastor is busy, but not too busy

The following conversation is typical of many I've had with church members over the years. The setting: shortly after the Sunday morning service.

'Kent, I just don't know what I'm going to do.'

'Well, let's talk. What about this afternoon or tomorrow?'

'No, you're so busy. I can't take up your time.'

'No, no, come on now. I've got plenty of time.'

'But you're so busy...'

'Yes, I'm busy, but never too busy to talk to you.'

THE GOAL of this chapter is to present the nature of what it is a pastor does. Pastors are busy people; this much is certain. I would not have known this had I not been one for the last four decades. Congregations can be better equipped to support and encourage pastors if they understand what it is they actually do, day to day. And, they can know that, despite the busyness, pastors are not *too busy*.

This chapter more than others is highly autobiographical — points are illustrated from my own experiences. Though I could rely on the lives of other pastors for anecdotal material, out of respect of the need for confidentiality, I bare my own soul and circumstances.

Additionally, I am writing with the small church in mind. During the 1970s, while pastoring a medium-sized church, the day to day work was similar to what I am presently engaged in, but I was not nearly as busy then as I am now at a smaller church.

What does a pastor do?

Study and preparation take up the bulk of my time and are the most difficult and labour-intensive part of the work. I study and prepare for: one, the Tuesday night Bible study; two, the Sunday morning sermon; three, the Sunday evening sermon; and four, the weekly local television program. Maybe, since study and preparation demand such a great deal of time and effort, that is why Paul wrote that those who labour in preaching and teaching must be accorded double honour. And, maybe *double honour* means appreciating and guarding the time needed and the effort expended by the preachers and teachers.

As a pastor of a small church, I am also janitor, administrator, secretary, groundskeeper, building maintenance person, and a doer of sundry other activities that must be handled each week. What a project it is when I go away on a vacation! It takes weeks to prepare to leave for a week and a week to catch up when I return.

Long ago I learned that it was not efficient for me to take an entire day off each week. That merely postponed things and required constant catch-up. Accidents, illnesses, and a myriad of other emergencies frequently come up and vie for my attention, along with the dozens of details that must be considered in the life of a busy church. Now I work part of each day, and can at least keep up. With a cell phone in my pocket, I am constantly accessible — I field many phones calls each day. If it gets to be too much, I can always turn the phone off.

Counselling was a major focus of my work. After all, my background is in psychology, and I left a graduate program in counselling to attend seminary. Now, I do not present myself as a counsellor, but there is still much time spent in pastoral counselling. In addition there are various other activities: weddings, a workshop for divorced people, funerals and memorial services, working with the preschool that rents space from the church and my volunteer football and baseball work at both San Quentin Prison and the local high school. I consider it vital to work out regularly at the local gym, something I have done religiously since 1978. Then I have a family with two teenaged daughters. It is a busy life, and everybody in the church knows it. It can make them hesitant to ask for any of my time.

Delegating

'Delegate' is advice I have received hundreds of times over the years. This well-meant counsel is partially legitimate, and I do delegate to the extent I can. Over the years, however, I have learned it is far easier to do many things myself than it is to seek someone else to perform the tasks. I have expressed this many times and am often challenged about it. It is simply that people don't understand what really happens. Let me give a concrete illustration.

On Saturday mornings, I rise early and am at one of our local grocery stores to pick up items that will be discarded that morning. It is good food, but the shelf time has expired — fruit, bread, cookies, cakes, pies, and other quality food, all for free. This is a job I would rather not do. Saturday is the one morning I would like to sleep in and enjoy just being at home with my family. But if I am not at the store at 7 a.m., the food will be destroyed.

I once arranged for someone to do it for me while I was away, and it turned into a small disaster. Yes, I would love to delegate this job, but to whom? If asked, many would volunteer, but most would not be able to do it consistently. There are several of these little jobs that are easier for me to do myself.

Too busy?

Yes, this pastor is busy, but again I say, not *too* busy. Some things can be delayed, postponed or neglected for a period of time. It may be that I'm the only one who knows I'm not too busy. I love to work, and I focus my attention wherever the need is. But, the squeaky wheel always gets the oil.

It doesn't take an emergency to talk to the pastor

My dear old friend Mark Buckley reminded me to say something about how pastors love to get to know their people and spend time with them — and it need not take an emergency for this to happen. Mark said that Jesus spent more time with Peter, James and John than he did with the multitudes in need. Yes, pastors love investing themselves in others, getting to know them, answering questions, helping them grow and simply building relationships. Mark is right, and as I considered his suggestion I thought back on my time at Miller Avenue and recalled so many times of just being together with members of the congregation, working on projects, doing fun things — time well spent indeed.

Christian friend, don't let this chapter give you the impression that the pastor is too busy to spend time with you, even when you don't have a problem to deal with.

In summary

It is vital that church members understand the lives their pastors lead. Since their lifestyle is quite different from the norm, it might be unknown or misunderstood. On the one hand, the church might think the pastor is too busy; on the other hand, the church might not appreciate the pastor's work because they don't know what goes on behind the scenes. Both extremes should be avoided.

One thing is clear, I could not perform all the tasks and ministries of even a small church alone. By God's grace, I am not the only minister in the church.

For further thought...

1. Do you know what goes on in the life of your pastor?
2. Is your pastor busy? Too busy?
3. What might you do to help that pastor?
4. How might you pray for your pastor?

seven

The pastor is not the only minister in the church

'Do you have other ordained ministers in the congregation, Kent?'

'Not right now. But we have licensed several people who cover for me at weddings.'

'Do you feel alone then; are you having to do everything yourself?'

'Not at all. For a small church, we have many who serve in important jobs. Sure, I am busy, but I am not alone. The Holy Spirit does gift people — this is a reality — and part of my job is to put people to work.'

LONG CENTURIES of institutional religion has produced a professional ministry, rightly or wrongly, with a division between clergy and lay people — the 'pros' and the 'amateurs'. (I try not to distinguish between clergy and laity in thought or word.) This is the dominant paradigm in the West at any rate — many churches have one 'professional' and paid staff member. But, it is never really the case that there is only *one* minister. God sees to it — he raises up and gifts others to do his work as well.

My goal in this chapter is to encourage people to work alongside the preachers, teachers and pastors, thus setting them free to focus on the primary work to which they are called.

Trained professionals

The church must have trained professionals. The work of preaching and teaching requires it. Yes, I have known those who never set foot in a Bible college or theological seminary and yet were outstanding preachers and teachers. However, without exception, these people were self-motivated, diligent students of the Scripture, people who sought out the best books on theology, church history, preaching, Old and New Testament studies, archaeology, philosophy and a host of other fields. *Self-educated* is the right word. People with a strong sense of call to a focused and concentrated gospel ministry must be equipped to do the work. But even they will not be what they could be without the empowering of the Holy Spirit.

Gifts of the Spirit

Listings of the gifts of the Spirit in Romans 12, 1 Corinthians 12 and Ephesians 4 make it plain that God intended to equip and empower *his church* to do the work of the ministry. Trained professionals make up a small percentage of the congregation but do a large share of the public ministry, especially in terms of preaching and teaching. But the job is far larger than that. Thus, the gifts of the Spirit are necessary.

A pastor does not have every gift of the Spirit. I may have three or four gifts, but that is all. The work I am unable to do or do poorly, others are gifted to do well. My favourite example is this: I do not like to visit the sick in hospitals nor make visits to people's homes. For four decades I have been this way. I do it, but I don't like to do it. However, at Miller Avenue we have a care team of about six people who love to do this particular work. Perfect. This is only one instance where people in the congregation are engaged in important ministry, much of which developed naturally, without my initiating it.

Discovering spiritual gifts

Early in my ministry, I used various techniques to determine what tasks people did well. That information, combined with data on personal preferences or desires, was meant to uncover spiritual gifts. Now I simply listen to people describe what they want to do or like to do, and then I observe what they actually do. Through a natural process, the identity of an actual ministry or gift begins to become evident. No labels or titles are needed to define a gift or job, instead I merely encourage people to create and develop a ministry inside or outside the church. Eventually, a significant percentage of people in our small congregation are engaged in some meaningful work.

One of my favourite experiences is to watch our congregation during the lunch that follows every Sunday morning service. These lunches are not small productions, and people take turns preparing them. Besides the cooks, there are servers and those who clean up. Quite a number of people are involved, and it is this I love to watch — ministers of the church doing the work. Recall Acts 2:42 where Luke describes the primitive Jerusalem Church and read about 'fellowship' and 'breaking of bread'. This is pleasurable activity, which fits in well with one of my main rules: *Try not to do anything that is not fun.*

There are potential problems

I don't mind being the primary preacher, teacher and pastor, but I know I'm not the only minister in the church. If I were the only one, my ministry would be inadequate and the congregation neglected. But with many people doing ministries in the church, there can be some problems. Certain jobs I will always do myself, even when I suspect others would like to do them. I retain these because it is easier for me to do the work myself. Either doing the job alone is more time or cost efficient, or preparing someone else to do the job is not possible; or, it might be setting people up for failure.

Every member is a minister

The church is filled with ministers. Indeed every member of Christ's church ministers to God through praise and prayer, obedience and love. We receive ministry, and we give ministry. God has made this possible through the work of the Holy Spirit. The Spirit is the Enabler — he who works all good things in us. And he enables us to minister as we freely yield ourselves to him.

Under the Old Covenant, only the priests, the prophets and kings experienced Holy Spirit anointing that enabled them to be ministers of the Lord. But prophets like Jeremiah were shown a day in the future when God would write his law on the heart of each of his people, 'for they shall all know me, from the least of them to the greatest, declares the Lord' (Jeremiah 31:34). This has happened. God made provision that his children would be enabled to be, and in fact are, ministers of the gospel of Jesus Christ! The church is full of ministers.

Paul wrote, 'Having gifts that differ according to the grace given to us, let us use them' (Romans 12:6), and, 'to each is given the manifestation of the Spirit for the common good' (1 Corinthians 12:7). Let us use our gifts, and use them for the common good. The pastoral leadership will be greatly encouraged by this. It will lighten the load and clear the way for the primary tasks of preaching and teaching. It is a concrete way to care for pastors.

My first pastorate

During my first pastorate, I did almost everything for the entire worship service. I am not exaggerating when I confess that most Sundays I prayed all the prayers (except the prayer for the offering), read the announcements, led the singing, sang the special music, preached the sermon and pronounced the benediction. There were many morning services when I stood up behind the pulpit at 11:00 a.m. and did not sit down again until I was in the car driving home.

Looking back on my first church, I realize I made several mistakes. One, I was overly impressed with myself — after all, I was a seminary student. Two, I didn't trust others to do the job right. Three, I never taught anyone else to do the work. Four, I did not teach that all believers were ministers. Five, I was ignorant of the way the New Testament church functioned. Six, the congregation let me get away with it, probably because they were afraid to confront me. Seven, those who had preceded me as pastor, did the same as I had done.

The errors were largely my own doing. The church may well have longed to be involved in ministry, but I was preventing them from exercising their gifts. Perhaps I didn't trust them, or rather, I didn't trust Christ in them.

Pastors and people working together

A word to leaders then is this: *Raise up people in the congregation to shoulder the work of ministry with you.* How would the battle have gone if Moses had not allowed Aaron and Hur to hold up his arms? Would Moses have been capable of judging the people rightly if he had rejected his father-in-law's suggestion? It is part of a leader's responsibility to *equip the saints* for the work of the ministry (Ephesians 4:12).

Saints must be willing to step out into areas that are unfamiliar and often reserved for the 'professionals'. Miller Avenue's Sunday morning worship service is a good example of what I intend. Besides the half-dozen or so people involved in the choir are the musicians and choir director. There are two or three worship leaders, people who preside over the offering and announcements, a leader of congregational hymns and one teacher and one preacher. Often I am not involved until it is time for the sermon. God, in his wisdom, pours out his Spirit and gives gifts to the church.

An all-inclusive command

The great commission of Matthew 28:19-20 was given to all the church through the twelve apostles. They were told to make disciples of all nations, baptize them and teach them to observe all Jesus had commanded them. Isn't that a staggering commission? Can a few do that? Jesus gave this all-inclusive command to *all* his church, and it takes all the church to do it. Every Christian leader who tries to do it alone will fail. Every church that thinks its leaders will do it alone is failing and forcing failure upon the leaders.

Who are the ministers? The believers are the ministers. Who are the leaders? People whom God calls out from among the ministers. Pastors, minister to the ministers, equip them for ministry and pray for more ministers.

For further thought...

1. What ministry would you like to do in the church?
2. What ministry needs doing in the church?
3. Is there something you could do that would lighten the pastor's load?
4. Is there a ministry in the church that you think would be fun to do?

eight

The pastor leads a complicated life

My resumé would look something like this: evangelist, pastor, preacher, teacher, conductor of weddings and memorial services, counsellor, author, student, janitor, landscaper, carpenter, landlord, exterminator, plumber, painter, roofer, administrator, stock broker, insurance salesman, private investigator, blogger, secretary, choir member, caterer, accountant, workshop leader, baseball coach, football coach, husband, father, grandfather, brother, uncle, friend and neighbour.

The good old days

AFTER MY second year of college, I joined the military. I ended up being a medic, but finished out my last two years of college during my four-year enlistment with the U.S. Air Force. Averaging forty-eight hours a week as a medic with 2nd Casualty Staging Flight at Travis Air Force Base in California, I attended college full time, had a wife and two young daughters — yet I considered it easy going.

During my seminary days, before I was pastoring, I worked as a psychiatric tech and sold shoes at a J C Penney department store. While I was a street preacher in the Haight-Ashbury District of San Francisco, I worked in construction half time for my father-in-law. During the Jesus Movement era, I supported myself by painting houses. Some of the painting days were hot, and the work was hard. I recall standing high up on a ladder for hours at a time, often in the heat of the day, painting under an eavestrough with an oil-based paint as sweat dripped into the paint bucket and sticky oil-based paint ran down my arm. That was miserable! Often though, I look back on those days with a genuine fondness and actually wish I could return to those 'good old days'. All I had to worry about was where the next job was coming from.

Painting was simple compared to pastoral ministry. There were bids to prepare, painting to do, cheques to collect, and then off home at the end of it. Simple. I could put up with the hard work for the uncomplicatedness of the lifestyle.

At seminary, I began to get a glimpse of the real life of a pastor. Still, school protected me from the full impact of the work. Many of us seminarians longed for the day when we would leave the books behind and settle into the 'comfortable' pastoral life.

Later, though still in seminary, I began pastoring a small country church. Due to the distance from our seminary apartment, I could only be with the people on weekends. It was less than a part-time pastorate, but I was in a much more involved situation. People were sick, dying and sinning, and I had to preach twice on Sunday. The work occupied my mind the entire week. I was indeed leading a more complicated life than ever before. When I graduated from seminary, I was faced with a choice: evangelism on the city streets or pastoring the church. I was glad God let me resign from the church.

Street ministry in San Francisco had its own complexities. Not only was there the problem of communicating Christ, but there was also the need to follow up with new converts. As the work grew, though it was para-church work and not an actual church, I was forced to function more like a pastor than an evangelist. However, those days were not at all what I was to experience as the pastor of a real church.

I had no idea

In September 1984, I began caring for a group of elderly people who remained after First Baptist Church of Mill Valley, California, closed. They had kept up hope for a new church to start. Though numbering only nine congregants, with an average age of seventy-five, we persisted and eventually opened a new church, Miller Avenue Baptist Church, on 1 July 1985. Twelve of us worshipped God that glorious Sunday morning. We declined in numbers after that, then grew some but fell back. One time we got up to eighty, then lost half of that and now have settled to about forty.

Regarding the resumé at the head of this chapter, I became all of those things. Today, I am still all of those things, except I gave up the private investigating, insurance and stock brokering work, mainly because I don't have time to do them anymore. When we began in 1985, I asked the church for permission to make money outside the church, and it was agreed, since it was abundantly clear that the little flock would not be able to pay a living salary. Because I loved the people and wanted to preach the gospel, I accepted a more complicated lifestyle.

Gospel preachers love the work and love to work hard, and so we complicate our lives. Miller Avenue Church knows about all I do, and they wonder about me and try to get me to slow down. I tell them I might, when I am dead!

This is the life of a pastor of a small church. I am writing this so that congregations will know something of the complicated lives their pastors can lead.

There is much to do

Much of my seemingly frantic activity is due to the fact that our small church cannot afford to hire a secretary or a janitor. There is much to do, but that is not nearly all of what a pastor faces and deals with.

Christian people, even the most faithful, can have an unreal idea of what the life of a minister is like. Consider the complexity of the Bible, the struggle to develop one's own theology and the tremendous responsibility to preach the gospel. This is coupled with the never ending job of teaching and equipping believers, administrating a church, with or without a building, counselling, ministering to the sick and dying, comforting the discouraged and caring for those who struggle with mental illness, which is a huge undertaking in itself. Then there are the issues: abortion, war, divorce, the end-times, the culture wars, the occult, secular religions, other religions, denominations, cults, social problems (drugs, alcohol, sexual perversions, poverty, homelessness), all of which are but a sampling of what confronts pastors on a daily basis. For me it means constantly keeping up by reading magazines, journals and books. It seems to me that Elijah, Peter and some of the other heroes of the faith had it easy!

Next come financial pressures — meeting the budget every month can be a constant source of anxiety. I am no fundraiser and have never preached a sermon on giving at Miller Avenue, but somehow God meets our needs. Still I fret. Worse are the requests I routinely receive for financial assistance, some of which are genuine and urgent. There is never enough money to go around, and far too often I can only plead, 'I wish I could.'

The extended congregation

In addition to the worshipping congregation, there is a much wider group to whom I minister. For many years we have conducted a divorce recovery and loss workshop. Many hundreds have been through this excellent program. Then, I have performed about 1,000 weddings while at Miller Avenue. Also, I have officiated at about 100 memorial services and funerals, most of these for families not associated with Miller Avenue. I have had a television program for more than twenty years — a verse-by-verse Bible study program — and, though it is only broadcast on the local community station, many people watch it.

All of this is to say that there are about four times as many people as the membership of Miller Avenue to whom I actually minister. These people do not regularly attend services; still there are the phone calls, emergencies, the need for my services and so on. It is regular and constant, and largely unseen by the congregation.

A day off

As I mentioned in a previous chapter, long ago I found it was not prudent for me to take an entire day off during the week. Many pastors take Mondays or Saturdays off. I have tried, but playing catch-up rarely works, because of people's needs and requests.

For over two decades I have made every effort to take afternoons off. Afternoons are when I write and coach sports, sometimes take a nap or read. If I don't take afternoons off, I end up working all day, since so much of what I do is in the evenings. What works for me is to wake up before dawn and start work immediately. By 9 a.m. the phone starts ringing and messages are popping up on my computer screen. My best study time is before 9 a.m. and after 9 p.m.

A hobby I love is gardening. I love my garden, but rarely get to spend much time there. It is a small patch, but even then I find overripe tomatoes hanging limply from plants I have failed to water. It is my garden's condition, and the lack of time I get to spend with it, that more than anything else makes me look longingly towards my retirement years and the hope of farming.

Living a public life

Pastors can feel as though they live, move and have their being in a glass bowl. Besides God, who knows how many other millions are watching (remember Hebrews 12:1)! The congregation is looking on, and the non-Christian world is always peering in. Additionally, I have nine different neighbours — some are families, some are businesses, plus there is the pre-school with all the teachers, parents and kids. One neighbour and I are currently at odds, and another causes me daily concern. And I have to be nice all the time. In Mill Valley itself I am somewhat known; some like me, some do not.

What can be done

Many people at Miller Avenue realize the varied pressures and problems their pastor experiences, and often they are able to assist. Simply knowing that they know helps. Knowing that they pray for me is a great encouragement, and seeing them enter as partners into ministry makes a huge difference.

I love doing what I'm doing, and no one can remove the complexities of life and ministry from me. Yes, there are the times when I have the sense that I am not getting the work done, that I am inadequate, even failing. This is when I need the church to be patient with me, accepting of my limitations, and understanding of a pastor's struggles.

I can empathize

To survive in our area, a very upscale community where moms and dads often both work, involves constant stresses and pressures. My own life helps me understand the complicated lives of others in the congregation. So many live hurried, complicated lives — I understand and can empathize. If I lived differently, I would have difficulty relating to others and they to me.

Congregations can understand something of the complicated lives pastors live, because the goals, dreams, visions and missions of a pastor and his people are so closely related and interconnected.

For further thought...

1. Do you know much about your pastor's daily life?
2. Did anything in this chapter about the lives of pastors shock you?
3. Are there other complications that I have failed to mention?

nine

The pastor is vulnerable

'Kent, do you think that was a demonic attack?'

'It could have been; I am not certain. I used to label anything that troubled me or the church a demonic event. Now I am not so sure, but whether demonic or of human origin, I hope never to go through something like it again.'

MODERN ARMIES train soldiers as snipers whose mission is to concentrate on high-ranking enemy officers. It makes sense to attack and destroy the leadership of the opposing force. With the generals gone, the troops might become disorganized and unable to wage war.

Spiritual warfare

Destroying leadership is strategically sound. Christians fight a spiritual war that is more complex and dangerous than any physical battle because it is not fought 'against flesh and blood, but against the rulers, against the authorities, against the cosmic powers over this present darkness, against the spiritual forces of evil in the heavenly places' (Ephesians 6:12). Though the gates of hell shall not prevail against the church of Christ (Matthew 16:18), though Jesus has soundly defeated Satan at the cross (1 John 3:8), still there are battles. Despite the fact that this warfare is largely invisible, without discernable front lines, with the enemy blending into the landscape, the ultimate victory is assured.

However, both world history and personal experience reveal that individual battles have been lost. In fact, battles fought by the church today or in any age are greater in magnitude, from God's point of view, than the notorious battles of the twentieth-century's world wars. This is so because spiritual battles have eternal consequences — heaven and hell are at stake.

What does a demonic attack look like? I am not sure, but sure only that I rarely see it coming and only see it, usually, when the battle is over, win or lose. I have lost some battles, and I have needed the medics in the congregation, perhaps with the spiritual gifts of service, exhortation, contributing, leading, mercy, wisdom and knowledge, to help bind up my wounds, get me off the battlefield and help me live to fight another day.

Our churches — open to attack

From the adversary's vantage point, every assembly of Christian believers is an enemy stronghold that must be reduced if he is to carry out his rebellious and murderous battle plan. Satan, of course, targets leadership. Pastors are obvious targets, since they are not behind the lines but are up at the front, hopefully, leading a spearhead into enemy territory.

All of us, however, leaders or not, engage in spiritual warfare, and well did Paul advise us to 'take up the whole armour of God, that [we] may be able to withstand in the evil day, and having done all to stand firm' (Ephesians 6:13).

The devil attacked Jesus

The devil tried to prevent Jesus from completing his ministry. As far back as Genesis and the Garden of Eden, there are stories of spiritual warfare. In the aftermath of the Fall — the rebellion of Adam and Eve — God said to the serpent, which the devil had possessed: 'he (the offspring of the woman, or the Christ) shall bruise your head, and you shall bruise his heel' (Genesis 3:15). Jesus Christ would deliver a deathblow, 'bruise your head', while Satan could only 'bruise his heel'. And Satan did make every effort to bruise that heel. We read about one such incident in Matthew 4 and Luke 4. After Satan's failed efforts to tempt Jesus in the wilderness, Luke records, 'And when the devil had ended every temptation, he departed from him until an opportune time' (Luke 4:13). Satan had not succeeded, but he did not give up; he would look for other opportunities. Though I have not the space to present a detailed account, as I read through the Gospels, I discern various times when the devil seems to seek to thwart the work of Jesus, often trying to get to Jesus through the apostles. One time Jesus had to say to Peter, 'Get behind me, Satan! You are a hindrance to me' (Matthew 16:23).

If the enemy could have gotten to the Head, the mission would have been tragically compromised, even ruined, but Jesus was without sin and withstood every attack through perfect obedience to the Father and reliance upon Scripture.

Wolves, sheep and shepherds

Jesus is the Good Shepherd who laid down his life for the sheep. A hired hand, one who does not own the sheep and, therefore, not truly a shepherd, flees when the wolf comes and leaves the sheep open to attack (John 10:11-13). Paul, while saying farewell to the elders of the church of Ephesus, warned: 'After my departure fierce wolves will come in among you, not sparing the flock' (Acts 20:29).

Who is the wolf? Whether demonic or human, the wolf attacks, and the under-shepherd, the pastor, stands in the way at the door of the sheepfold. To get to the sheep, the wolf may attempt to jump over a wall, but still the shepherd comes running. The best plan is to force the wolf to deal with the shepherd first. Strike the shepherd, and the sheep will be scattered and then devoured piecemeal.

Wolves have succeeded

Many a wolf has gotten into the sheepfold. Many a shepherd has been attacked, many severely harmed. Who cannot recount a story or two? I can tell you, and sadly, of wolves ravaging shepherds and sheep. Satan is not toothless yet. Defeated yes, but he is still the god of this world (2 Corinthians 4:4) and the prince of the power of the air (Ephesians 2:2). How all of this works I don't know, but I can give ample testimony that it does.

The art of polishing and refining

Satan is not the only source of attack upon the shepherd and the sheep. There are rebellious ones in the fellowship itself who trouble those in spiritual authority — often unconsciously. I have been one of these rebellious ones, without realizing what I was really doing.

We are all growing up into the fulness of Christ, pastor and congregants alike. Part of growing up is going through the rebellion that we often associate with the teen years, though in this context it is spiritual rebellion. Rebellion may be too strong a word. Maybe it should be referred to as the normal and natural movement from spiritual immaturity to maturity. Certainly, some advance gracefully through it; others go kicking and screaming. It can be very wearing on pastors, especially on those who do not understand the process of spiritual maturation, and likewise it can be confusing to church members. Some will not appreciate the dynamic and fail to grasp the 'grinding' or refining process taking place.

Christian leaders are like grinders who polish rough stones.

God uses people, particularly those in spiritual authority, to grind off the edges that need it most. This process may produce conflict and pain. The Lord is a purifying God, and he uses pressure to heat things up. When the heat is on, there may be complaining, but the end result is worth it.

The shepherd, as well as the sheep, must understand that shepherds are in a vulnerable position. Pastors and congregations must know the devil will attack and that people will act out as they 'grow up' in Christ.

The offence of the gospel

The good news we preach is good only to those who have been rescued from the wages of sin. Those who are committed to their sin will hate the gospel and the gospel preacher. They will sometimes take irrational means to silence the preaching.

In our sin we are haters of God and goodness, rebels against the very God who loves us. Where will that hatred be focused? Very often, at the preachers and teachers of the church. And the hatred can be fierce. In my second pastorate, the church fought a terrific battle against some fortune-tellers who wanted to open up shop in our town. Many in the congregation were involved in gathering petitions, attending city council meetings, praying and writing letters. But in articles that appeared in the local newspaper, I was the one the occultists attacked. Threats of violence were made against me, and a stone came sailing through my bedroom window late one night. As the pastor, I was in a vulnerable place, the one most open to attack.

The ordinary criticisms

Strange charges, without basis, are made against pastors, most of which come from outside the congregation. Those that come from within are even more hurtful.

Since the work of pastors is public and open, their every word can be examined. And I have learned that no one will measure up; no one will please everyone all the time.

As a baseball coach, my decisions on the field are constantly evaluated. Over the course of a ball game, I make dozens of decisions, and not all are going to be successful in accomplishing the goal. When my hunch doesn't pay off, there is criticism. I can't avoid it, but it can hurt, especially when the criticisms are used to undermine my authority and credibility. Many coaches become embittered and resentful; some quit.

Leading a congregation is similar to coaching a sport — errors are made, plans and programs flop. Here is where the congregation must be alert to the vulnerability of their leaders who may feel the heat and begin to question their own ability. They may become fearful of doing much at all and fail to lead; in addition, they may become angry, bitter and resentful.

Critics are common, criticizing is easy, and most of us are good at it. We tend to be less skilled in encouraging and lifting up. When most people would criticize, the Barnabas types in the church (Barnabas means 'son of encouragement') have the opportunity to build up and strengthen their pastors. *This may be the single most important way a congregation can care for church leaders.*

Avoiding a cultic mentality

There may be times when a pastor has erred and sinned. Though a pastor is in a vulnerable position, a spiritually alert, loving congregation can provide a shield and covering. This does not mean a political style cover-up like we hear politicians involved in. Sinful behaviour cannot be covered over, but care must be taken for the good of the church as a whole. Where there has been the breaking of the law, pastors must be held accountable. Whether the offence is moral or criminal in nature, a congregation cannot neglect its duty to Scripture and society. The principles of Matthew 18:15-17 need to be observed. Forgiveness, reconciliation and the glory of God are the goals.

Watch and pray

Preachers and teachers will be wounded — this cannot be prevented. Empathy for the wounded leaders by the church family goes a long way towards healing. To be understood and appreciated, to have the sense of being loved and cared for — this is the balm that heals. The Great Physician so often shields and protects, comforts and encourages, forgives and heals — all through his Body, the church.

Churches, keep watch and be alert for the wolf. Stand with the shepherds and their families when the long-standing battle flares up right in front of you.

For further thought …

1. What is it to be vulnerable?
2. What may preachers and teachers be vulnerable to?
3. Have you known a wounded church leader? Was there ever healing?
4. How can a church stand alongside their pastor?

ten

The pastor has a family

'Kent, what about you starting a class for new believers?'

'You're right, we do need one. It won't be a big class, but definitely enough new Christians have begun attending to justify it.'

'You have Monday evenings free. Every other evening is taken up.'

'Right, I guess that is the only time I have left.'

'PREACHER'S KID goes bad' — something close to this headline is occasionally seen in newspapers. I think everyone has read a few of these articles. There has even been a book or two written with a similar theme and at least one song that I can think of. Yes, the pastor's son or daughter who stumbled and fell — it does happen.

Usually the trouble is blamed on an overly-religious upbringing.

During my twenty-six years volunteering at San Quentin Prison, I have run into a few preachers' sons. Some ministerial colleagues of mine have told me stories about their families that were difficult to hear. I know a number of pastors who have been through divorces, and I also know of suicides.

Sad stories about pastor's families are often told with either an 'ah hah' or an 'I could have told you' attitude. For non-Christians, such stories may serve to cement them in their unbelief. Some Christians will even delight in hearing tragic tales, especially if it is about a pastor in a denomination different from their own.

Pastors have families

Pastors have the usual and normal experiences of family life like anyone else. However, all too often, the pastor's family is expected to be perfect. Paul wrote that a pastor or elder must manage his family well (1 Timothy 3:1-7). But Paul does not clearly describe what that looks like. Could it be that in the first-century, children were, in general, obedient and perfectly mannered? Often the standards applied to a pastor's family can be so rigorous that no family would pass inspection. I have seen it just that way.

At a breakfast not long ago, I was with some pastors and missionaries who belonged to a particular fellowship of churches that were proud of how they cared for each other's families. The adults had supervisory authority over any of the children in the fellowship. These were all young families; none of the kids had reached their teens yet.

I suspected that the future for these families would not be as smooth as the parents hoped. As I listened to the account of the supervisory strategies they had for their children, I thought to myself how glad I was that I was not closely involved with them. Kids being raised by a group of adults, however compatible and 'on the same page' the parents thought they were, might well suffer as they grew up.

By the grace of God, none of my children rebelled and ran

amuck; in fact, all have turned out to be more wonderful than I sometimes suspected they might. Today, all my children are believers and active in their churches. My three oldest, married with children, along with their husbands and wife, are faithful Christians. For this I will always thank God.

Churches do not parent the pastor's kids

I made a concerted effort to shield my kids from having to conform to the expectations of some members of the congregations I have pastored. That said, it is also true that congregations can be a source of great encouragement to pastors by being supportive of their families. For instance, never once has the Miller Avenue congregation, either corporately or individually, attempted to criticize, correct, admonish or advise my twin daughters, now age eighteen. What a relief! In fact, my daughters, I am sure, will look back on their childhood, living in the church's parsonage, as a very blessed and special time.

The second of the three churches I pastored was different. There were busybodies in that church who would give me books, tapes and so on, thinking they would help me raise my family. One associate pastor gave me a book about how to cast the demons of lust, lying, cheating, disobedience and so on, out of my three children. I resisted these efforts, as politely as I knew how. I learned early on to be protective of my family and would not allow anyone in the church to start telling my wife and me how the raise our kids. The old saying, 'Mind your own business', is wise counsel indeed!

Families — a source of anxiety

I have often experienced guilt and anxiety about my family. Occasionally, someone will say, 'You're so busy; you don't spend much time at home, do you?' The intention might be good, but it hurts nonetheless. When I hear this sort of innuendo, I cringe. Maybe it is caring and not blaming, but I can't tell the difference. The result, too often, is that I suspect I am failing and that I am a bad father and husband. I am reminded of 1 Timothy 3 and think that maybe I shouldn't even be pastoring a church at all. Even if I knew that I spent a reasonable and normal amount of time with my wife and kids, I'd still feel guilty.

The family — living in a fishbowl

I am aware that I live in a kind of fishbowl, and so does my family. Something happened during my oldest daughter's first year in junior high that caused me considerable anguish. I was at the school's open house and Dory, my oldest, was showing me around the school. At one point she led me out into the hall to show me her locker. Lettered on it in white chalk was, 'Jesus freak'. She giggled a little and quickly rubbed it off. I asked, 'Dory, what was that?' She said, 'Just some kids.'

That startled me. It felt like I had been kicked in the stomach. I felt responsible, and I hurt for Dory. I didn't like it that she had to take all that pressure and abuse. I asked, 'Does that happen often?' Her reply made me feel even worse. 'Yes, all the time.'

'All the time? Oh no!' I started getting mad. I wanted to know, 'Does anything else happen?'

A lot happened. Name-calling, taunting, rock throwing, exclusion, whispering and rumours. A great deal of abuse was directed at a thirteen-year-old simply because she was my daughter.

This was very discouraging to me. For days I couldn't shake it and became so upset that I thought of getting out of the ministry. Dory was suffering because of my work, and I felt bad.

While few pastors want the congregation to get involved in their family's lives except in the normal give and take of the worshipping community, even fewer congregations know anything about the price a minister's family pays.

The family as a ministering team

Congregations sometimes can expect the whole family to be doing ministry. I overheard a conversation in a seminary cafeteria three decades ago that upset me so much I still remember it. One student was bragging, 'You know, we got that whole family for only $1,000 a month.' What he meant was, his church had just called a new pastor, and he felt like they had hired the whole family.

I don't like the idea that a pastor is hired and serves as an employee in the first place, but I like a lot less the idea that all the family members are employees. Some of them may indeed find areas of service in a church, but it must not be expected, anticipated or demanded — it must be the family member's own choice. And if this occurs, they must not be held to a higher standard than anyone else. Wives and children of pastors may live and serve in an exemplary manner, but they must be accorded the same considerations as any volunteer.

Pastors and their families — ordinary people

We are all sinners, imperfect people in various stages of spiritual, emotional, physical and intellectual maturity. This applies to pastors as well as their families. Being sinners, pastor's families need ministry like anyone else. It is possible that pastors might neglect their families, not intentionally, but due to the pressure of events. I have found that I am at fault here — taking care of everyone in the church and forgetting those closest to me.

Some pastors need help themselves and do inflict various kinds of injury on their families. It is my experience, though, that most pastors love their families and want to minister to them to the best of their ability. Every pastor will be as keenly aware of 1 Timothy 3:4-5 as I am: 'He must manage his own household well, with all dignity keeping his children submissive, for if someone does not know how to manage his own household, how will he care for God's church?'

I take that passage seriously. If my home is out of order, the church may be also. These words of Scripture are the express will of God, yet, does it demand perfection? Does it mean that there ought never to be any problems in the pastor's personal flock? Being a pastor does not mean that being a parent and a spouse is easily done.

The church is number three

Every pastor's primary responsibility is to God; his family is number two. The church is third, after God and the family. Isn't that true? Isn't that what 1 Timothy 3:4-5 teaches? Church, do you know that you are number three?

One evening, years ago, I got a phone call from a couple in our fellowship who asked me to visit their close friend in a hospital some distance away. The woman in the hospital was going to undergo serious surgery the next day and wished to have communion. She specifically wanted a visit from me. Visiting hours were strict, and I would have had to leave for the hospital almost immediately.

Normally that would have been no problem. The Philpotts, though, were just walking out the door for a movie that was a birthday present to my second daughter, Grace. It was a rare event for the whole family to go out together.

I knew what a disappointment it would be for my family had I headed off to the hospital. As best I could, I weighed the factors. I stuck with my family; we went to the movie, but I felt guilty the whole time for not going to that hospital.

When I said I could not go but would visit their friend the next afternoon, this particular couple did not understand. They complained over the phone, and swore they would not have me for a pastor. They made good on their promise; I never saw them again.

Pastors are always on call

The job of shepherding never ends. There are no set hours, and emergencies continually arise and often at the worst possible time. Pastor's families have to cope with this uncertainty, not unlike the families of medical doctors who are on call. There have been vacations, short or long, that had to be rescheduled or truncated due to illnesses, deaths and other emergencies. Life and reality happen, and pastors share the lives of the congregation. Pastors are always on call.

Therefore, churches can help their pastors by letting them put their family first and do it in a way that generates as little guilt as possible. When there are family problems, congregations can give support in prayer and understanding. Helping pastors minister to their families ultimately means that pastors will be better able to minister to the whole church. We are to build one another up, not tear one another down.

For further thought . . .

1. Have you been supportive of the pastor's family?
2. Do the family members work for the church?
3. Can you think of something you might do to encourage the pastor's family?
4. Do you pray for the pastor's family?

eleven

The pastor may become spiritually bankrupt

'From the pinnacle of success, into a near black hole, he fell and was consumed by the darkness.' This headline is from a newspaper reporting on the spiritual and moral collapse of a well-known pastor.

And we all shudder.

AS UNPLEASANT as it may be to contemplate, congregations must be aware that pastors can become spiritually dead inside. I have had this happen to me, and one of the predisposing factors to spiritual decline is physical and emotional exhaustion.

The nature of the work

Everyone who labours with body and mind becomes fatigued. Pastors of small churches, out of necessity, work with both body and mind. But even if a preacher delivered only one sermon a week and did absolutely nothing else, the preparation, thinking, reflecting, praying, and the actual preaching itself are not an insignificant amount of work. It is my understanding that thirty minutes of standing and delivering a sermon is equivalent to four hours of physical labour in terms of energy spent. Probably the stress involved in public speaking accounts for much of the energy drain. Regularly standing before a group of people, in season and out of season, is not easily done.

Sermon preparation is a creative process. Having to come up with 100 different sermons a year is wearing and stressful. Then having to preach the sermons, and preach them well, to a congregation expecting great things from the pulpit, is not easy to do.

Thinking is one of the most intense forms of labour humans engage in, and preachers and teachers must be thinkers. Without the discipline of constructing hundreds of outlines for research papers while in college and seminary, my work would be almost overwhelming. Being experienced in developing outlines is one thing, but carefully working through the Scripture texts, which can be quite complicated, requires considerable mental acumen and energy.

Preaching twice on Sunday, and everything else that goes on during the course of the day, almost always completely exhausts me. Though I keep fit, still play sports and exercise three times a week, Sundays are real work. But as a pastor of a small church, I work seven days a week, and I can tell that I am not as strong and able as I used to be.

Pastors are also counsellors. Professional counsellors and therapists are aware that their job can be exhausting. Ten appointments a week can be a full workload because of what the counsellor puts into it. Though they are not lifting boards and bricks, counsellors give of themselves intellectually and emotionally. A day of pastoral counselling can be as draining as a day digging a trench.

Communicating is one of the most complex of all skills, and pastors are communicators. Among the highest paid people in our culture are those who engage in some form of communication, whether that be in television, film, theatre, writing, classroom teaching, and the list goes on. We are so accustomed to work being physical that we fail to see the full picture. Communicators themselves may not be aware of the implications of their labours.

Wrestling

Counselling, sermonizing, studying, planning, visiting, praying can drain a person. Besides physical, emotional and intellectual, there is spiritual energy. While this is almost impossible to calculate, it must be considered. Paul spoke of *wrestling* with or against spiritual powers (Ephesians 6:10-20).

Note the word 'wrestle'. Then as now, wrestling is incredibly physically demanding. Let me state unequivocally that pastors wrestle, and this is spiritual work, unseen, most often unspoken, but work that goes on constantly.

The point in all this is that pastors spend or exhaust themselves both physically and emotionally, and this may lead to a spiritual breakdown.

A personal confession

There have been times in my ministry when I've gone for weeks without praying, except on Sundays or at Bible studies. I said weeks, and I should have said months. (For some pastors it has been years.) No one guessed my condition. However, the well was empty, and I didn't know what to do to refill it. I was spiritually bankrupt. It was something I felt, a kind of sadness that wore me down.

Sunday became the most dreaded day of the week. I figured there was nothing the people could do about it anyway, so I quietly kept going. When I occasionally expressed how I felt, the reaction was not helpful but only added to the trouble. Like the soldier of the cross I hoped to be, I tried to move forward, all the while hoping for better things to come.

My sermons were poor during those times; the Bible studies were flat. I avoided meeting with people for pastoral counselling. I couldn't find a good sermon topic or a passage from the Bible I wanted to preach on. Usually I preach with conviction and a confidence that what I am preaching is what God wants. But in those bankrupt times, I was forced into getting out old, and by that time, dead sermons, to preach. Those were hard times. Could the people tell? If so, they rarely let on.

Feeling desperate

Life in the ministry can become desperate. Some pastors have acted out so as to get themselves fired just to relieve the stress and pressure. This has happened to very solid Christians who knew they were genuinely called of God to preach the gospel of Christ. No one is immune. Everyone is vulnerable.

Pastors of small churches can be especially stressed because of the demand for success, which usually means a growing congregation and budget. Whatever fruit the church growth movement produces, the struggle to be successful has not been a blessing to any but a few. If our emphasis had been on getting people into the pews and dollars into the offering plate, Miller Avenue would have looked like a failure — that is, *I* would have looked like a failure. Surprisingly, perhaps miraculously, I did not feel this particular pressure, because my congregation did not put any such pressure on me. I was just glad to be able to have a church at all and to be able to preach and teach, if only to a few.

Some years ago, I understood that I was called to be faithful and not successful in worldly terms. It has not mattered to me that some denominational leaders had other bottom lines in mind. Had I been pressing for worldly results, had I begun to take personally the need to constantly increase the 'nickels and noses', I imagine I would have resigned long ago.

When people are under great pressure for sustained periods, what do they do? We know some of the answers, since they are amply illustrated for us in the daily newspapers. As a volunteer at San Quentin Prison, I know what bizarre means people take to deal with that which threatens to undo them. Pastors, like others, living busy, vulnerable and complicated lives, may go bankrupt in every possible way.

A visit from a friend

One of my seminary friends suddenly appeared at my door some years ago. I had not followed him in his ministry, and due to the passing of the years, I did not recognize him at first.

Cautiously, he began to question me about how I dealt with feeling spiritually worn out. It seemed an aimless conversation, and I began to be impatient until he abruptly confessed he hadn't prayed or read his Bible devotionally for nearly a year. I leaned forward, looked into his eyes, and told him I understood. Then the dam broke.

He talked about the standard problems in the congregation, unrelenting financial struggles, his wife's medical problems, and the fact that he had nothing stored up for the future. He had no way out, no way to survive without the church, and this made him resentful. Besides, there was the typical but crushing pressure to preach or teach two to three times a week. He had no close friend in the church, and he didn't want to further burden his wife by complaining to her. So he came to talk to me.

He was doing badly, and the knowledge of his failure and the people's accompanying comments had nearly led him into deep sin. The spiritual and emotional burdens were heavy — a yoke he was carrying alone. He was close to hating the church, himself and the pastoral ministry. He was bankrupt.

There is danger

Many pastors who have been in their positions for a while, know and understand the struggles of this pastor. It is one thing to be tired; it is quite another to be spiritually dead. If a leader is not in close fellowship with God, ministry can be awful. Paul was concerned that even though he preached the gospel, he might himself be disqualified (1 Corinthians 9:27). It is difficult to know exactly what Paul had in mind, but it seems to be close to the subject of this chapter.

Paul exhorted Timothy, 'Be sober-minded, endure suffering, do the work of an evangelist, fulfill your ministry' (2 Timothy 4:5). He would not have said this had it not been possible to be and do the opposite. What Paul said to Timothy he says to all. It is not beyond the realm of possibility to preach and teach, give and give, work and pray and end up being disqualified for the ministry.

A crisis of faith

Can a pastor struggle with his faith? Yes. Now there are two possibilities here. One, there was no genuine faith in the first place, only a false conversion. This is not as rare as it might seem. In my book, *Are you really born again?* (Evangelical Press), I deal with this issue at length. There is faith, and then there is faith that comes by the grace of God in regeneration. The two may look similar at first, but life events will expose the weakness of faith that comes only from the heart and mind of an individual. After youthful idealism, the strength of emotional/spiritual experiences and pressure from other people and institutions run their course and lose their power, there may be no real biblical faith at all.

Two, true faith implanted by God may be present, but the stress and turmoil of life can nearly, but only nearly, reduce that faith to the point of crisis. My experience, both personal and anecdotal, shows me that genuine faith, however crushed, will not be snuffed out but will grow again.

Congregations will not likely be able to distinguish between the two. Time will tell the story, but in any case, the church is called to prayer, patience and love.

Another view — a spiritual plateau

All Christians are growing from glory to glory. One glory level may seem like a dead end when it is really a plateau, a springboard, or maybe a resting place prior to another growth spurt. Parents are familiar with growth spurts in their children, growing two inches in a few months, then a period of less noticeable or no growth. Spiritually, people also grow in spurts. At the tail end of a period of spiritual maturing, Christians can experience a plateau and feel as if God has left them alone. A sense of spiritual bankruptcy may suddenly ensue.

Whether the circumstance is a plateau or a spiritual bankruptcy, the question should be: *What can the congregation do for the pastor?*

The congregation helping to prevent bankruptcy

Isn't rest and recovery built into the pastor's work? Won't the pastor's normal, daily devotions prevent a spiritual and emotional decline?

Most often, the normal spiritual disciplines in which Christians engage do go a long way towards preventing real trouble. But they may not. There is mystery here, one which will not yield to quick and easy answers. There is no shortage of self-help books written on the subject. Obviously, these books serve their purpose, as there are so many, but experience tells me that what they offer as solutions are not a sure thing. Reading a book, listening to a CD, going to a conference, receiving some counselling, doing a retreat, taking a sabbatical break — all of these are practical means of healing and restoration. But they are not guaranteed solutions.

How I see it

Let me speak from the heart. This is a most delicate issue. The subject matter seems so disconcerting that I thought about deleting this entire chapter. Yet, it is so very important; congregations must face it. Christians do go through difficult times, pastors included. In Christ, through the ministry of the Holy Spirit and the fellowship of the saints, are the resources to effect healing and renewal. With confidence then we don't shy away from troubling issues.

I will personalize this and offer what I hope my church would do if I go through another spiritual wilderness.

One, give me time. Don't give up on me. Poor sermons and dry Bible studies will trigger talk and suggestions, which I will consider, but experience shows me that I will come out of it. Genuinely talented baseball players go through times when they perform miserably, but they come out of it. The same applies to pastors.

Two, let me know I am loved and cared for, that I am prayed for. I can go through any struggle when I know others are going through it with me. God does walk with us through the valleys, and maybe one way he does that is to send a brother to walk alongside for a distance.

Three, do something tangible. Find a task I am doing and do it, relieve the burden just a little. It might be something simple, quick and easy, but it can mean a lot.

Four, speak about the reality of the spiritual and emotional troubles we all go through, which opens the door for frank discussions. Anxieties, fears and temptations are stripped of their power when we get them out into the light.

Five, there may be instances where nothing will prevent a slide into bankruptcy, and the best ministry a church can bring is to allow the pastor to fail.

For further thought...

1. Does it seem possible that a pastor would struggle spiritually?
2. What is the difference between correction and restoration?
3. What is the difference between condemnation and encouragement?
4. When you are spiritually and emotionally struggling, what helps you the most?

twelve

The pastor must be free to lead

'We feel that forming a softball team would be too risky. We haven't enough youth to make it work anyway.'

'I have talked to a number of people who want to do it. It would be a lot of fun, too. And, you know that new family that has been visiting, they gave me the idea. He coached softball at the high school level, and he and his son plus his wife are all softball players. We can do it.'

'Pastor, you've forgotten about insurance and other possible costs — we are just too small to do it right.'

IF I HAD BEEN the pastor in that scenario, I would not have been encouraged. (Over the years, I have played on many church softball teams, and they proved to be a wonderful way of involving new people.) Here was a ready-made opportunity, and one fearful person might derail a special interest the pastor had to lead the church into a new ministry. What difference does it make if there is a failure? There is no learning to lead without risking failure.

Leaders fail. Failing is not the problem; *failing to lead* is the problem. A church must give their pastor permission and encouragement to lead. Some pastors have little trouble being a leader. However, most pastors struggle with it. It must not be assumed that an effective preacher and teacher will be a strong leader.

I consider myself an aggressive leader, yet I have been so beaten down at times that I wanted to crawl into a shell and not make another decision. Certainly, I am a risk taker, and not too afraid of failure, but I can be intimidated into inaction if I lack my church's encouragement to move forward.

A pastor-led church

Several styles of church government have some biblical warrant. Generally speaking, there are episcopal, Presbyterian and congregational forms of church government. The first is top down leadership with an established hierarchy; the second is leadership by a group of proven elders; and the third is democratic in nature — one member, one vote. In a sense, Miller Avenue combines all three of these forms of church government. Some of the members say it is a pastor-led church, and I don't argue with the description. It may not be the best form of church government, but it is what developed at Miller Avenue.

How it works at Miller Avenue

Miller Avenue Church has given me permission to be their leader. They gave it to me because, over the years, despite some spectacular failures, they learned to trust me. The church steps in if it is felt that I am headed in a wrong direction, but it must be obvious.

Our mission is to preach the gospel to non-believers and to teach the Scripture to believers. If what I am doing meets these goals to some degree, then I am given the support and encouragement of the church.

We do not vote on anything. Ideas come up and are talked about, and if a consensus is reached, then we proceed. I set the agenda; anyone can bring up anything, and we toss ideas around and attempt to make sense of them.

It is my responsibility to bring people into leadership positions, including paid staff. The whole church must be involved in ordaining anyone to pastoral leadership, but aside from that, I make the selections and decisions. The church does not tell me with whom I must work closely.

The preaching and teaching in the church are my responsibility, as is the worship and all that goes with that. My aim is to conform to biblical models and accepted church tradition.

We have always had sufficient finances, although there is no pledging, capital fund campaigns, or other mechanisms to get people to give. I don't know who gives what, only the treasurer does, and I don't care to know. People who understand the mercy and grace of God and who take the great chapters on Christian giving seriously (2 Corinthians 8 – 9) will give generously without being asked to.

Whatever the form of church government — and a pastor-led church like ours is not uncommon — the congregation must give the pastor the encouragement and support necessary to lead.

God's anointed?

'Touch not my anointed ones, do my prophets no harm!' (1 Chronicles 16:22) This verse, from a prayer of King David, made a huge impression on me as a young Christian. I understood it to mean that pastors should not be challenged or opposed. It set the pastors apart, and I felt as though they were to receive the utmost honour and respect. I had no idea that some pastors may not be good pastors and even less of an idea that they might even be bad.

There are pastors who are called of God, and there are those who are not. This is common knowledge, but even those called by God may have difficulty. Some may fall, and fall miserably. Ordination is not magical — no invisible, spiritual shield descends on the ordained. No pastor is to be followed blindly. A pastor must be biblical and faithful to be a leader in the church. Godly leadership primarily means being a good and faithful servant.

The leader is a servant

The pastor is the servant of the congregation who serves primarily by preaching and teaching. Every other service is important but secondary in comparison. The pastor may lead in worship, prayer, praise, evangelism, administration, comforting the wounded, caring for the poor and so on. The pastor is actively engaged in the work and brings others into the work in a partnership mode. The church allows the pastor to be its servant and encourages that service.

Freedom to lead

We have launched a communication ministry to local Muslims. An Imam has visited our church and explained Islam to us. Our hope is to engage in direct dialogue with Muslims and have the opportunity to explain what we believe as well as continue to learn what Muslims believe. We believe in the power of the preached gospel to save.

Additionally, we are opening a branch of Homosexuals Anonymous, where those who understand that homosexual behaviour is sinful and want out of the gay life can find some support. (We are ten minutes away from San Francisco, California, one of the centres of America's gay population.)

As leader of the congregation, I talked about, over the course of several months, what it might mean to engage in these ministries. We talked about the potential for trouble, even danger, and we became aware of the risks. But we are also aware that outreach is what we are called to — we are to preach the gospel to whomever we can. Despite the possible trouble and danger, the church is allowing me to lead us into these new ministries. If I had encountered serious objection, I would have reconsidered. To go on when people I trust are in substantial disagreement would mean I would gradually lose my ability to lead.

The abuse of power

Power is corrupting — this is beyond dispute, and we are all prone to abusing power. People new to the pastoral ministry may find themselves suddenly empowered and exhilarated by their potential to control situations. Now they have respect and influence, real power, and it can be intoxicating. The result may be good, or it may be evil.

It might seem that I am advocating that a church should give permission for a pastor to lead without regard to good sense. Pastors can, in fact, act foolishly and destructively. Rather, it is better for a pastor to earn the right to lead, and prove his leadership is biblically sound and appropriate. Churches can reach a stage of burn-out, and this usually happens where a pastor has abused power or used the church to advance a personal agenda that is not in line with the basic mission of the church.

Courage to give permission to lead

Freedom to lead is a precious gift churches give to pastors — more so when churches have been damaged by pastoral leadership. There are failures, and then there are failures. A church may have to summon great courage when a pastor begins to be an aggressive leader, especially if they have been abused in the past. Though Miller Avenue is a pastor-led church, I can still be removed at any time, or people can 'vote with their feet' and simply leave.

Churches, whether they have had bad pastoral experiences or not, must allow pastors to lead. There is something wonderful that trust conveys to leaders — it can refine, inspire and sanctify. It is better to encourage pastors to lead than it is to seek to control them. It would be better to find a new pastor than to attempt to control or squash pastoral leadership.

The mission of the church requires sound and true leadership, and where there is good leadership, there are also failures.

For further thought…

1. What do you think of leaders as a whole?
2. What would it mean to respect leadership?
3. How might leaders be encouraged?
4. What should you do when your leaders fail?

thirteen

The pastor must be free to fail

'I've decided to get a teaching credential and hope for a job in a high school, maybe in the English department.'

'You are going to resign then?'

'If I don't, my family, as well as the church, will suffer. Kent, I think way back at the beginning I let myself be talked into going into the ministry. I made a mistake, and now it is time to correct it. This last failure finally woke me up.'

THIS CHAPTER is about three kinds of failing: one, failing at specific ministries; two, becoming burned-out; and three, leaving the pastoral ministry altogether. Each year, many pastors experience one or more of these.

Rather than attempting to outline specific remedies for each of the three areas where failure can occur, I decided to deal only with general principles. Churches are so different from each other and particular instances are so varied that I do not want to suggest any dogmatic way of dealing with failings. I am depending on the spiritual maturity of Christians to apply appropriate biblical principles to their own circumstances.

Attrition rate

There is a certain attrition rate in the pastoral ministry — one that I suspect is higher than most people might imagine. Some of my classmates at both of the seminaries I attended did not go into the ministry at all after graduation; some went on to ordination and service in a church only to leave after a few years. Others spent many years in ministry, but left due to burn-out or a moral or mental breakdown.

The same can be said of any vocation. Medical doctors, dentists, psychiatrists, corporate executives, attorneys, scientists, politicians and so on fail and have to change careers. This is far from uncommon. Some failures are more dramatic in their consequences than others. We read about some of these in the newspapers, but even under the worst of circumstances, the goal is recovery and restoration.

Specific ministries will fail

Like many churches, we had an outreach to youth. It continued for some years but then it ended. A member of the church came to me wanting to know why we had not planned to continue it. At first, I thought he wanted to be involved. His real concern was something entirely different. He said, 'It must not have been God's will.' Not continuing a ministry meant for him that it could not have been God's will in the first place. 'Why didn't you know it wasn't God's will?'

Was this an accusation? Was it a theological question? Was he disappointed that now he would not be involved? Could he have been thinking that if something was God's will, it should continue for ever?

To me it was simply that the outreach had ended. For one thing, the leader had gone away to college, and I could not find a replacement. Then too, the number of kids involved had radically declined. Clearly, the work had ended; the outreach had, in a sense, failed.

The questions emerged: Might we fail? Are we allowed to fail? Does God demand success? Is failure sin?

Am I a failure?

Over the course of forty years of ministry, with dozens of efforts at evangelism, missions, discipleship and outreach to the poor, many, if not most, ended in some degree of failure. Some achieved initial goals; a few completely flopped. Money was, unhappily, wasted on some occasions; once we ran afoul of the law. But we always worked with faith and zeal. As best we could, we followed what we had understood to be God's will. Yet we failed. We had taken risks and experienced failures.

Risk taking is an important element of ministry. We don't look into crystal balls to ascertain the future. We move ahead by faith, and that means risk. Even if our faith were perfect, risk taking is not eliminated.

After one of my more infamous failures, I was tempted to be cautious, even fearful. It is unpleasant to stand before a church council meeting and explain why an outreach failed after some real money had been spent. To squander tithes and offerings is serious, and it can plague me for years afterward.

People wonder why some churches do so little and seem so inwardly directed. Could it be that their leaders are afraid to step out and risk failure? Occasionally I've felt that it would be best to have a morning service, a mid-week prayer meeting and nothing else. Fewer risks yield fewer criticisms and a more peaceful life.

Not long ago, we closed a Bible study headed by a young man. It turned out to have been a mistake, though not a tragedy, and we all learned from it. Would it have been better not to take the risk? From my point of view, no. Others disagreed, and there is no way to determine the truth one way or the other. We took a risk and it did not work out. Should we never take risks?

A couple of decades ago, the movie *The Omen* came to town. Some of our braver folks stood outside the theatre and handed out flyers I had written. One of the members of our fellowship commented, 'What if someone is offended? We'd better not do it.'

Yes, someone might be offended. (Someone always is, you know.) Yet, the possible benefits were good, and the risk needed to be taken. Fear is a great weapon that Satan uses against us. Timid leaders are not able to direct the church into areas of ministry where people are profoundly affected by Christ. Where a congregation fears failure and avoids risks, the pastor will have to leave or yield to the direction the fellowship wants to go.

Churches must give their leaders the opportunity to fail. The Holy Spirit often inspires spontaneous ministry and opens unique doors of outreach. These may look risky, and probably are, but giving pastors freedom to step out into unknown areas of Christ-centred projects is essential. If failure comes, evaluation is fine, but not recriminations. The deadly threesome of 'woulda, coulda, shoulda' must be avoided at all costs.

Burn-out

Burn-out has become a cliché and is often used for spurious motives — almost as something to hide behind.

'My problem is I am just too tired and discouraged to carry on.' Is this burn-out or something else? Perhaps 'stress' is a better word. Stress — that tightness of body and mind that reflects our inner state, that inability to relax and take it easy, that pressing and straining that almost becomes our normal state of being — is closer to what I mean. A sense of being driven by deadlines, events and expectations of others, or the animal type of survival instinct — these express the elusive nature of burn-out. That we can come to the end of ourselves emotionally, spiritually and physically is all too obvious.

According to Scripture, people are to work six days and rest one day. Certainly, the expected length of the work week has fluctuated over time. Some are accustomed to the five-day work week, some to a four-day work week. Where I live in Mill Valley, California, many normally work six days a week. I work some part of all seven.

The principle is that we are to rest and not work all the time. We need to rest; that is the way we were made. If God rested, we ought to. Of course, I think that the biblical picture of God's resting is a looking forward to our resting in Jesus Christ who rested from his labour and is seated at the right hand of the Father. I rest then in the finished work of Jesus, but my body and mind need rest too. Though I work seven days a week, during a part of each day, I attempt to rest. My resting may be working in the garden, working out at the gym, taking a nap, coaching football or baseball at the high school or at the prison, spending time with my family, reading a good book, watching television, listening to music — the list goes on. The point is, I rest because if I don't I will pay a big price. That price, for lack of a better word, is burn-out.

Burn-out sneaks up on us. Like a heart attack, there may be some indications of trouble, shortness of breath and chest pains, which are often ignored or attributed to something more benign — indigestion or that hot chili pepper at the Mexican restaurant. Usually, we carry on and keep going.

Something will give, eventually. It may be a display of anger, a lingering malaise, undefined and undiagnosable illnesses or difficulty concentrating. For me, the symptoms are blurred vision, loss of interest in the preaching and teaching, not looking forward to the gatherings of the congregation and insomnia.

It is not uncommon for people in the church to see signs of my distress before I do. One or two know me well enough to talk to me about it. Surprisingly, that is a major factor towards my recovery. Merely being able to talk about my feelings does wonders. Another reliable measure of my well-being is the fun factor — if I am not having fun, something is wrong. I have a rule: the pastor, or the coach, depending on which hat I have on, must be having fun. 'Fun' is a strange measurement, but a helpful one for me.

Pastoral burn-outs come and go and do little real damage unless the congregation is not able to absorb them. This is not a call for a close scrutiny of pastors or a constant pulse taking, simply an awareness that pastors, like anyone else, may be going at it too hard and can get into trouble.

There is trouble, but then there is trouble.

Leaving the pastoral ministry

When I leave Miller Avenue, there will be sadness for me and the congregation. It will be a loss, and grieving will follow. It is unavoidable. Those leaders who come after me can be sensitive to the loss and minister to it. I hope to visit my beloved people and be available by email and phone. But my leaving will, overall, be a good leaving.

Pastors will leave, not of necessity or due to failure, but because it is simply time to move on. Many denominations have transitional or interim pastoral leadership — it is understood from the beginning that their time with the congregation is limited. These pastors understand when their work is completed and move directly into another ministry. There might also be loss and grief with this leaving, but it is not generally severe.

What about pastors who have determined they should not be in the ministry at all but need to do something else entirely? What about pastors who have experienced a moral or emotional/mental collapse that cannot be resolved or corrected? At this point the ministry can legitimately be said to have failed.

Failure is something we would rather never experience. However, failure is a part of life. Pastors fail; they are vulnerable to moral and emotional/mental collapse despite having been saved by grace. I have seen it over and over and experienced it personally to some degree. What now? How does the congregation respond to this kind of failure?

First, there are the pastors who come to an understanding that they should not be in the ministry any longer. Perhaps these pastors sense that they made a mistake in the beginning, for whatever reason, and now want a correction in direction. Or, they have come to a place where they see that they don't have what it takes to do the work.

I have known pastors who were never able to overcome the anxiety often associated with public speaking. Some could not adjust to the chaotic and demanding schedule or lifestyle of a pastor. A few developed illnesses that made it almost impossible to be an effective church leader. One veteran pastor told me of being unable to continue to bury people and visit the sick in hospitals. Another pastor had to leave the ministry because it was simply too troubling to his children. I could go on and on with this paragraph and never cite all that I have seen and experienced.

Perhaps, and this is not unheard of, pastors see that they are not even Christians and do not hold to the doctrines of their church. This would qualify as an essential reason to leave a congregation.

Without recrimination and with kindness and gentleness, congregations can allow the necessary changes to take place so that the memories everyone takes away are pleasant, and in the end, God will be glorified.

Second, there is true and obvious failure. Whatever the reason for the failure, and an emotional/mental collapse is every bit as difficult to deal with as a moral issue, let me say that it is of greatest importance to acknowledge that pastors are members of the household of God and therefore need to be treated with kindness, gentleness and respect — despite the failure. God will deal best with his children; he will judge and discipline.

Christian leaders have done the most incredibly stupid and rebellious things; and yet, often years later, these same people proved to be fruitful in the kingdom of God. It has become clear to me over the course of my ministry, that some failures serve as a refining fire — dross is consumed and precious metal purified. Another analogy is a runner in a race. We only see a snapshot of a moment in time and not a video of an entire life's race; we do not know how a person will finish the race. We may see only a stumbling along the track not a recovery and strong finish. A patient and compassionate congregation can be instrumental in bringing renewal and restoration. I have witnessed the same.

Of course, I have seen the opposite, where a failure merely exposed a deeper flaw that had to be excised. A congregation may have to protect itself and take action for the good of all. Even still, this must be conducted with respect and Christian *agape* love. That love also needs to extend to the pastor's family.

If a pastor fails and must be removed from ministry, there may be a family to be considered. Some years ago, a pastor embezzled money from his church and ultimately went to prison. The family was given a month to vacate their home, and no other help was offered. The family was not guilty, only the pastor, but four others, including children, suffered. Additionally, in the congregation were those who did not respect the action of the church's elders and left for another church.

The goal of a congregation must be the glory of God and the well-being of the church family, along with the recovery and restoration of those who have failed. What congregation is sufficient for these things? Failure, especially immoral and criminal behaviour, incites so much passion, outrage and hurt, that many congregations are unable to deal effectively and helpfully with the trouble. Things sometimes go badly; God's honour suffers and innocent people are damaged in the process. This is often the case and is the reason for this chapter. May it be that God is glorified in his church.

For further thought . . .

1. What do you feel like after a failure? In those cases, what has helped you and what has harmed you?

2. Have you ever experienced burn-out? How did that happen and how did you recover?
3. How have you reacted to the failure of ministries and ministers?
4. Outline a strategy for dealing with the three types of failures mentioned in this chapter.

fourteen

The pastor needs enough money

During my second pastorate, my daughter Grace needed a bicycle. She didn't press us for one, but my wife and I knew she'd love to have one for getting to and from school.

At that particular point we could not afford one, there was no pool of money to draw from, and I had no credit cards even if I had been willing to get into debt. In a moment of weakness, or honesty, I don't know which, I thought, 'Does anyone care?'

I knew God cared, so I prayed to him. He loved us. Did anyone else?

NOT BEING able to pay the bills or provide for common family needs is as disheartening to pastors as to anyone else. I haven't seen God's people begging bread, but I have known pastors who could not adequately provide for their families.

A testimony

My testimony is that God has in fact provided for my family and me. Within reason, I have lacked nothing. Many times it did not look like there would be enough, but there always was, sometimes miraculously. During the years of the Jesus Movement, 1967 to 1972, there were miracles, and I will retell one of these.

One morning in 1968, while living in San Rafael, California, my family of four, plus two other young adults who shared our home, were gathered for breakfast; there was nothing to eat and only tea to drink. We asked God to take care of us, and before we finished the prayer we heard a knock at the door. Two people, whom we had never seen before, were standing on our front porch holding white styrofoam containers full of scrambled eggs, bacon, potatoes, toast and milk — a substantial breakfast for exactly the right number of people. These two people, a man and a woman, left immediately before we had a chance to thank them, and we never saw them again. Had we entertained angels without knowing it?

That was one instance, and there were many others. Most were less dramatic, but I have never doubted that my Father in heaven was watching over me.

Enough to get by

'Ministers aren't supposed to be rich; they need just enough to get by.' This type of thinking is all too prevalent. Pastors may be expected to live at a lower standard than others in the community. The idea is: 'God will take care of them.' And this might well be so, yet I have found after years of experience and from the witness of Scripture, that God's provision essentially comes from, or should come from, the congregation. God may use miracles like that cited above, but the normal process of meeting the needs of preachers and teachers is through the agency of the church.

During my first pastorate, I never made more than $20 per week, which did not cover the cost of the fuel for my 300 miles of weekly commuting. From my second church, I received a maximum of $800 per month and put in at least sixty hours per week as senior pastor. In neither church did I make 'enough to get by'. Instead, I survived on the grace of God, and a monthly newsletter.

Pastors don't punch a time clock and do not work regular office hours. The typical ministerial responsibilities are unusual compared to common work norms, so mental and emotional adjustments must be made in order for pastors to accept themselves as workers and providers. Pastors are not making sales, building cabinets, painting walls and so on; pastoring is 'people work', and more than that, it is *spiritual work*, which is intangible and nearly impossible to outline in a job description.

It could be that out of a sense of guilt or a misunderstanding of the nature of the pastoral life, pastors themselves have sometimes accepted the idea that they only need just enough to get by.

Bi-vocational

Many pastors of small churches will be bi-vocational; that is, they will earn money working in jobs like I have — house painting, construction, insurance sales, stock brokerage and so on. Some bi-vocational pastors feel like failures when their churches are not able to supply what is necessary to provide for their families. Some churches feel badly that their pastors have to be bi-vocational.

When I came to Miller Avenue, I requested that I be given the freedom to work outside the church. I was, I do and I enjoy it — and I have not felt like a failure. The congregation has not felt badly that I have earned money outside the church. Of course, this work has complicated my life to some degree, yet it has provided wonderful opportunities for witness and ministry.

Not placing a burden on the church

Our denomination conducted a study regarding the potential for

Miller Avenue's church growth. It indicated that Miller Avenue would likely remain a small church, primarily due to severe parking restrictions. Therefore, it has been my intention that undue financial pressure not be placed on the congregation. I took a modest salary and some medical and retirement benefits and have avoided salary increases all these years while receiving small increases in benefits. With the income I have earned from secular work, plus the money my wife has earned by teaching sewing our needs have been met. Our church has always had enough money to do all we need to do. We have never had an emergency meeting about money. (The surrounding community even suspects we might be wealthy!)

Every year the church council wants to raise my salary, but I resist, not for foolish pride I hope, but the Philpotts have no debt and live somewhat like other Mill Valley families do. We have enough, and we are grateful both to God for his care and to our small congregation for being so generous.

My circumstances, however, cannot necessarily be duplicated for other pastors. My wife and daughters are healthy, as am I. We enjoy living a simple life, and our outside work has paid off. I don't intend for my particular experience to be a guide for how every small church should treat their pastor. Rather, it is better to see what the Word of God says.

Pastors and money: what the Bible says

Scripture has some plain words to say about money and ministers. In Luke 10:1-11 we read the story of the sending out of seventy-two men to preach the gospel. Jesus did not want the thirty-six teams of two to take money with them; rather, the households that received their service were to meet their needs. He said, 'Remain in the same house, eating and drinking what they provide, for the labourer deserves his wages' (Luke 10:7).

'The labourer deserves his wages.' These are the words of Jesus. The work of preaching the kingdom of God should produce income. The preachers were not engaged in a business, but their work was so vital that their living needs were to be taken care of.

The seventy-two would not be living the high life; they would be living like those to whom they ministered. Preaching is usually a full-time job, and there is not enough time and energy to focus on making money the standard ways.

The product of the pastor's labour is intangible. The work may not bear fruit for years in the future, but the benefits of the work are incalculable. The labour consists of obedience, faith, commitment, love, loyalty, honesty, pure intent, watching, praying, preaching, comforting, suffering, humiliation and so on. It is hard work.

The tentmaker

Paul made tents to produce income. At times, he did receive gifts from churches, but exact details of his financial support are not entirely known. Paul's calling was unique. Pastors may not live the same way as Paul. Nowhere is it written that pastors should emulate Paul's lifestyle, though some will, by choice or revelation. There is every indication that those called of God to work in his kingdom will do so under normal living circumstances and conditions. For instance, Paul spoke of the wrongfulness of muzzling an ox while it was treading out the grain. The Law of Moses prohibited that practice; God was watching out for the beasts. Paul asked the Corinthian Church, 'If we have sown spiritual things among you, is it too much if we reap material things from you?' (1 Corinthians 9:11). A return on spiritual investment was expected. Corinthian believers owed Paul their eternal lives, in a very real sense. He had evangelized, taught and pastored them; it would not be unreasonable to receive some financial support from them. (We learn, however, from 2 Corinthians that Paul did not desire to receive money from the Corinthians — and did not.)

Paul asked the Corinthian believers another question: 'Do you not know that those who are employed in the temple service get their food from the temple, and those who serve at the altar share in the sacrificial offerings?' (1 Corinthians 9:13). In the following verse Paul's teaching brings us to the point I want to make: 'In the same way, the Lord commanded that those who proclaim the gospel should get their living by the gospel.' Notice, 'get their living' not 'minimum rations'. Does God especially bless poverty, or does God love us more if we are poor? The ministers of the gospel are to receive their living from the gospel work itself. Those who benefit from that work are to share their material resources with the preacher/teacher. This biblical principle is honoured, upheld and commanded in both the Old and New Testaments. Additionally, the giving is to the Lord and not people, but people benefit. When I give money, I see myself ministering to the Lord even though the money may go to purchase cleaning supplies or new hymnals or be used to pay a church leader's salary.

Pastoral expectations

Most pastors don't expect or desire to live in luxury. Congregations are not required to see that pastors live in luxury either. Faithful Christians, including pastors, live a rich life in many ways — the richness is in Christ! But pastors should not have to worry about feeding their family and paying the bills. The congregation is responsible for seeing to those things. It is greatly to the benefit of the church to do so, for it frees pastors, in terms of both time and peace of mind, to do the work of preaching and teaching. It is difficult to preach and teach when basic and common family needs are not being met.

What might be done?

Church family — be sure that those who labour among you receive an adequate income. As you are able, see that the income covers the basics, and there is 'fun' money, too. It is not a luxury to be able to take your family to dinner occasionally and to go on a vacation. Consider also what the pastor will do when he retires.

If there is not adequate income for the pastor, speak of it openly and brainstorm to find other means of meeting needs. Give the pastor and/or his wife freedom to work outside the church. Examine the church budget to see if anything can be cut out or reduced to put that amount towards the pastor's salary.

Be understanding and patient with the pastor and his family when financial crises come along. And pray that God would provide what is needed.

For further thought…

1. Does it seem reasonable that pastors should have an income from their work?
2. Must pastors be poor? Must they be wealthy?
3. Is it embarrassing to talk about money in the church?
4. Who is likely to benefit from making sure the church leaders receive enough money?

fifteen

The pastor will be angry

'I remember the time you walked out of a church council meeting.'

'Yes, I remember it too, but I don't remember why I was so angry.'

'Really, Kent? Somebody challenged you on a budget item that you wanted. You weren't getting your way so you just up and walked out. We were all shocked. Then, later on, you had to come back into the meeting because you needed that budget passed.'

That was not a good day.

THE KIND and gentle pastor leading the sheep to peace and pasture — this is what we would like to see, and this is what we do see most of the time.

A natural emotion

Anger is an emotion given by God for our well-being. Anger is a protective device, like the sensation of pain; it gears us up to action when we are threatened. Anger, however, may be dangerous, since it can lead to sin and serious criminal behaviour. Uncontrolled anger might be expressed in a destructive manner and directed at others or ourselves. Repressed anger can turn into anxiety, depression, suicidal thoughts, dangerously high levels of stress and more.

Pastors can be angry.

Jesus was angry

Jesus attended Sabbath worship at a synagogue in Capernaum. A man with a withered hand was also present. Others in attendance wanted to see if Jesus would 'sin' by healing the man on the Sabbath. Healing was considered work and strict religious observance dictated that no work, including healing, take place on the Sabbath.

Jesus asked, 'Is it lawful on the Sabbath to do good or to do harm, to save life or to kill?' (Mark 3:4). There was no reply. Mark then reports, 'And he looked around at them with anger, grieved at their hardness of heart' (verse 5).

Now consider the scene at the temple in Jerusalem. Was Jesus upset and angry when he drove the money changers out of the temple (John 2:13-22)? Of course! It was righteous anger because his Father's house was being desecrated.

Unrighteous anger

All pastors' anger is not righteous. None of us is Jesus. We are people, members of a fallen race. This is not asking for license to be sinfully angry. Neither should we give up on ourselves because we are not as perfect or as mature as we are called to be.

Jesus, in the days of his incarnation and living among us, was never angry to the point of sin. But I am a sinner, and though I do not want to, I can get angry, sinfully angry.

Frustrated rather than angry?

Maybe frustration, rather than anger, is the more accurate term. Frustration is common, as anyone who works closely with people knows. Pastors deal intimately, continually and strenuously with people. Few others work with people on the level and intensity that pastors do. The social worker, doctor, psychiatrist or parole officer, none of these normally enter into a person's life to the depth the minister does — cradle to grave, and all the stops in between. Pastors experience the crises of life, the full range of everyday troubles. And that means frustration.

Caring and anger

My son Vernon, while a little boy, darted out into a busy street after a football. I yelled at him, 'Vernon, don't you do that again!' He cried and ran home to mommy. I could tell by the way he looked at me that he was angry with me. I yelled, and I was upset, because I loved him.

There are good reasons to become angry; there really is such a thing as righteous indignation. Some of Jesus' anger may have been motivated by love and thus could be said to have been righteous indignation. I would like to think that caring for individual members of the congregation has generated some of my anger. Compassionate anger, though, can easily be misunderstood. Combine frustration and caring with a sense of responsibility, and there is a potential for displays of anger.

Pastors will be angry about sin as they have ample opportunity to see the deadly cancer that sin is in the lives of people. Jesus was angry about this as well, angry to see what sin did and angry that others were leading people astray and into sin. On occasion, I have intervened in the lives of people who were in the process of destroying themselves. It has not always been pretty, and I have sometimes been angry in those situations. The detached professional I am not, not when it comes to the people I am responsible to care for. A time or two my anger crossed boundaries; I lost some measure of control. Remember: pastors are people and in the area of emotions, are not unlike everyone else.

An unavoidable source of anger

Anger is a normal part of the loss experience. When there is loss through death or divorce there will be anger. In fact, when we lose almost anything — a job, a home, a physical ability, a friendship, a prized possession, the list is a long one — there will be anger to some degree, depending on the significance of the loss. Often, the more we have loved what we have lost, the greater will be our anger.

Anger due to loss is normal and will not be put off. Denying or repressing our anger prevents recovery from the loss and will manifest itself in other, more dangerous, ways.

Pastors experience loss on a regular basis and rarely realize their losses. When I first came to Miller Avenue, the congregation of about nine elderly and wonderfully faithful Christian people were worried that I would leave them because our church was so small. They told me directly that they hoped I would be there to bury them. And one by one, I did. And each time I experienced a loss. Someone I had learned to love left me, as well as leaving the whole church family, but to me it was personal. For some of these dear people, I was there when they died. As I write this, I can see all their faces before me. Though some have been gone for twenty years now, I still miss them. I have carried this around all these years, and I have had many more losses.

People have occasionally left Miller Avenue Church in an unhappy fashion. Strangely, some who left were people I had poured myself out for the most. These painful losses in particular remain unresolved, which makes it difficult to recover from them.

Loss after loss, and I never have processed them, or not completely or effectively processed them, and the result is I carry some normal and natural anger around in me. I am aware of this, but I don't know what to do with it, even after leading a workshop for over twenty years on how to recover from loss. I have anger in me. It will come up from time to time; sometimes the anger is accompanied by a deep sadness.

It is clear that pastors are candidates for anger simply due to the nature of the work — being close with people and losing relationship with them for any number of reasons. I am not shocked that pastors carry around unresolved anger in them. How could it be otherwise?

Pastors have tempers

Just as there is *righteous* indignation, there is also *unrighteous* indignation. I have had my share. Pastors can have tempers. Remember the story of my first pastor, in chapter four, who chased the Mormon second baseman through the outfield with the intent of inflicting great bodily harm? He was mad. He was not crazy, just mad. He was wrong; he was human; he embarrassed us all — but he was our pastor, and we forgave him.

Did I say I walked out of a church council meeting? Well, I did it twice, I am sorry to say. Both times my anger was inappropriate and completely wrong. I took some heat for it, but most people never said a thing about it. Indeed, a couple of dear friends went out of their way to let me know I was still loved.

How a church can respond

Pastors will be angry and will embarrass themselves and others. Yes, church families, you may see your pastor inappropriately angry. What to do then? To make it simple: Do to others what you would have them do to you. How do you hope to be treated when you do something stupid? Though there may be some variation, from strong discipline to loving acceptance, we still know what we need.

The Scripture says we are to love one another and forgive one another. This is for everyone, pastor and congregation. Pastors forgive sheep, sheep forgive sheep, and sheep forgive pastors.

For further thought ...

1. Is all anger sinful?
2. When is anger acceptable?

3. Have you seen a church leader act out with anger?
4. How would you like to be treated if you acted out with anger in front of your church family?

sixteen

The pastor hopes to enjoy the work and find satisfaction in it

'A big reason I am a pastor is that I love it. Almost every day I wake up and look forward to the work. I'm having more fun now than ever before. For all these years at Miller Avenue, I have looked forward to seeing each of your faces on Sunday morning, which is why I stand at the front door and hand out the bulletins. My greatest pleasure is standing at the pulpit and seeing your welcoming and expectant faces as I open my Bible to begin preaching and teaching. I do live for this; how blessed I am to be able to serve you, my dear friends.'

The previous paragraph is in quotation marks. They are a fair and accurate composite of words I have spoken from the pulpit many times. The encouragement and love the congregation has given me over the years have etched these words of endearment on my heart and mind.

ALL OF US hope to enjoy our work and find satisfaction in it — pastors and church leaders included. This is basic and universal. For Christian congregations, the target audience of this book, the issue then becomes how to help pastors enjoy their work and find satisfaction in it. It is when pastor and congregation together are being built up and encouraged that the whole church brings honour and praise to God.

Our pressured, stressed and anxiety-ridden society has produced scores of unhappy and depressed people. Christians are not immune to this either. In my decades of ministry, I've come to know many pastors who find no joy in their ministry. These pastors, suffering for whatever reasons, pass their discouragement along to their congregations. Relationships become strained, people perform out of duty, not joy, and the fruit of the Holy Spirit — the love, joy, peace, patience, kindness, goodness, faithfulness, gentleness, self-control — seem to have vanished. In their stead are the works of the flesh.

In this last chapter, I hope to bring to congregations the awareness of the importance of pastors enjoying their work and finding satisfaction in it.

If it isn't fun, I am not going to do it

There should be quotation marks around the above statement; they are words I say frequently. A version of it is: 'The coach has to have fun. If the coach isn't having any fun then changes are going to be made.' This last statement I make at the beginning of each baseball season at the prison and at the high school. And, I actually mean it.

Maybe it is that I have lived long enough to know how important it is that I enjoy the ministry and the coaching. If I am not having fun, I will not do well, and no one else will be having much fun either.

Yes, I think fun is a theological word and a biblically correct category. I think Paul would have said he was having fun despite all he was living through. Fun, well, *satisfaction* then — Paul loved what he was doing. After all, he was serving his Lord Jesus Christ. To me this is fun; it is satisfying. The one thing I dread when I retire as pastor of Miller Avenue is the challenge of finding ways to serve the Lord. Here, service is built in for me. But later on, I might have to get more creative.

The 'whys'

Why would a pastor be discouraged? Why would a pastor not be satisfied in the work?

I do not know. Those who know me know I do not like 'why' questions, because they are usually of a blaming nature. 'Why?' is almost an accusation. I have wanted to say this throughout the book, and this is my last chance. Here is the relevance: I would be careful about asking a pastor a 'why?' question, especially if the pastor seems down and discouraged.

During the times when I've been discouraged, I cannot put my finger on a 'why'. There is generally a trigger such as an argument, a program gone awry, physical illness, financial woes or something else. Usually the distress is short-lived and temporary but recurring, sad to say. I'm not speaking of serious emotional trouble, though pastors are vulnerable to that as well. As I have attempted to make clear in this book, it must be understood that pastors will struggle just like anyone else. Simply because pastors are blessed to be in service to Christ does not mean that the troubles of being human and living in a world of fallen humans will not have an impact on them. Pastors don't wear invisible spiritual shields. Despite protective structures that may be in place, such as a pastoral care team, prayer warriors, an accountability process or the companionship of mature pastors both within and without the church, there are no guarantees.

Pastors do battle against the world, the flesh and the devil. Battles are lost, as we all know. A battle lost, or fought poorly, may cause a severe wound, since pastors tend to hold themselves to very high standards. One pastor I know abruptly quit when he fell back into drinking alcohol after many years in Alcoholics Anonymous. What for many would merely have been a bump in the road became shame he could not put behind him. Pastors often have very sensitive consciences.

We live in a comparatively comfortable society where many people learn to blame others for their problems. Then, as we grow up, both spiritually and emotionally, we rebel and act out towards authority — which includes pastors. Though a pastor may understand this behaviour, it is not pleasant, and after extended periods of time, it becomes very wearing and ultimately depressing.

Gospel preachers and Bible teachers offend people. It goes with the job. And the offended will often go on the offensive. As nice as I try to be, I will offend, and I will pay the price. Early in my ministry, I was surprised by this, and taken aback. Now I know better but still smart from it. I warn others about the dangers of preaching to rebellious Christians and non-Christians yet have trouble heeding my own advice.

A word from Peter

Peter encouraged elders, or pastors, to tend the flock of God *willingly* (1 Peter 5:1-2). The pastoral ministry was to be conducted willingly, not under compulsion. Do these words of exhortation indicate that Peter suspected some pastors may have been working without joy? He also instructed church leaders, in the same passage, not to be greedy or domineering. It may be that when pastors are not ministering willingly and joyfully, they fall into sinful behaviour.

Bible writers like Peter nowhere express the idea that pastors are perfect or that the pastoral ministry will be pure pleasure. The exhortations, to love, forgive, forebear, welcome, accept, receive, pray for, are for *all* the household of God, including the leaders of the church. Where the common Christian graces are extended throughout the Body of Christ, it is more likely that the pastors and elders tend the flock willingly, being examples to the flock. It becomes contagious, a mutual building up cycles through and through. The result is the glory of God in the church.

For the benefit of the church

It is for the benefit of the church that the spiritual leaders are able to accomplish their work with joy. Under normal circumstances, this will be the reality when the church is living for the glory of God. For our own good, and for the growth of the kingdom of God, we want those who minister to us to be doing it with joy.

For further thought . . .

1. What would be appropriate synonyms for 'fun'?
2. Is it reasonable that pastors should enjoy their work?
3. What might make church life 'un'-fun?
4. What might be done to make your church life fun?
5. Does it seem as if your church leaders are enjoying their work?

afterwords

First afterword

I HOPE not to create any degree of difficulty for pastors and congregations. It occurred to me that this book might trouble congregations by making them overly concerned for their pastors. It would not help to alarm congregations about caring for their pastors so that they would feel the need to hurriedly develop programs and strategies. This could become a burden beyond reasonable expectation. This in turn might lead to pastors needing, with some anxiety, to reassure their congregations about their state of being. Pastors prefer to go about their work without their needs becoming a focal point for the congregation.

My sense is that any insights gained from reading this book should be unobtrusively, slowly, even silently, implemented into the life of a church. To that end, I intentionally limited concrete suggestions on how to go about caring for pastors, teachers and other church leaders. Each congregation is different, and what might be helpful for one might not be for another. It is not my desire to have churches develop plans to facilitate ministry to pastors, but rather to help individuals within churches understand the nature of the pastoral ministry and then, in whatever means suitable and appropriate, put the caring into practice on an individual basis.

Second afterword

WHAT IS GOOD for the pastor is good for the congregation. It really is a mutual thing. The great and golden rule is, 'So whatever you wish that others would do to you, do also to them, for this is the Law and the Prophets' (Matthew 7:12).

Congregations are to love and care for their pastors; pastors are to love and care for their congregations. It therefore follows that the members of the congregation are to love and care for each other. This is understood.

My view has been that a book like this was needed because it is not always evident to many in the congregation that they *are* to love and care for pastors. I did not want this point to trump or overshadow the mutuality of loving and caring in the Body of Christ.

Other titles by Kent Philpott

Are you really born again?

Understanding true and false conversion

By Kent Philpott

Jesus said, 'You must be born again' and 'Not everyone who says to me, "Lord, Lord," shall enter the kingdom of heaven.' The most important question anyone could ever ask you is 'Are you really born again?' You need to know whether you are 'safely on your way to heaven' or 'sleeping on the brink of hell'.

Many people today think they are Christians, yet do not demonstrate any evidence in their lives that they have ever truly been converted. Too many of those who pass through evangelical churches and make an initial profession of conversion, or even are admitted to church membership, subsequently fail to manifest any evidence of a real and lasting work of God in their lives.

In the course of a long ministry as pastor in an evangelical church, Kent Philpott has acquired wide experience in observing and assessing people's response to the gospel. In this book he sets out principles which will be of great practical help to all Christians who are involved in any form of evangelism and at the same time challenges the reader to examine his or her own conversion experience.

> 'This searching book, examining true conversion, ought to provoke a much-needed and healthy rethink in the languishing contemporary church.'
>
> — *John Benton, Chertsey Street Baptist Church, Guildford, UK*

EVANGELICAL PRESS / EARTHEN VESSEL PUBLISHING
ISBN 978-085234-604-4

Are you being duped?

Find out before it's too late

By Kent Philpott

Are you being duped? How would you know if you are or not? Have you embraced ideas and concepts that are working against you? Do you believe you will simply die and that is the end of your existence? Do you really think all spiritual paths lead to the one true God? Do you think your life is all about *you* and your happiness? Have you really looked at truth for yourself or have you only bought into what influential people around you believe? Are you so bound by contemporary models of diversity and tolerance that you do not know what truth is?

Most of us want to believe in things that soothe our consciences or take the edge off our dissatisfaction with life — but they do not ultimately give us lasting peace, hope or purpose. Perhaps you do not realize you are buying into a lie; we seldom do.

Are you being duped? is a book about countering error with truth. It is about discerning what we are really embracing when we believe certain ideas or philosophies and what the culmination of them will be. From his own experience of being duped and through the teachings of Jesus, Paul and the other apostles, Kent Philpott confronts these errors, explores their consequences and then provides a biblical response to them.

If you *are* being duped and you do not realize it, this could be the most important book you have ever read.

EVANGELICAL PRESS / EARTHEN VESSEL PUBLISHING

ISBN 978-085234-557-3

From death into life

by William Haslam

'The parson is converted! The parson is converted!' was the cry from the congregation the day Rev. William Haslam was converted. It happened to this Anglican priest while he was preaching in his own church. This was in Cornwall, England, in the 1840s.

The Rev. Haslam tells the story of his conversion, and so much more, in *From death into life*.

Kent Philpott says: 'I have not had a book have such an impact on me in two decades; I have never seen so many people of my personal acquaintance so struck by a book in my lifetime. We simply wanted others to read this incredible story.'

EVANGELICAL PRESS / EARTHEN VESSEL PUBLISHING
ISBN 978-097032-962-2

For pastors of small churches

by Kent Philpott

Most churches are small churches and they are — and always have been — the backbone of Christianity, despite the emergence of the 'mega' church.

Kent Philpott, himself a long-time pastor, provides practical encouragement to pastors of small and large churches alike. Pastors around the world have found it to be a valuable resource. The emphasis throughout the book is that the one thing all pastors can do, is preach the gospel of Jesus Christ.

EVANGELICAL PRESS / EARTHEN VESSEL PUBLISHING
ISBN 978-097032-960-8

Why I am a Christian

by Kent Philpott

> 'Given all the barriers and obstacles that stood in my way I am surprised I became a Christian at all. There were so many hindrances that, thinking of them now, I am amazed afresh that I was ever converted.'

From this starting point Kent Philpott deals with the vital and pertinent questions of why and how we become Christians. Pointing us to the mercy, grace and divine sovereignty of God through every trial and difficulty on a Christian's road to salvation he answers such questions as 'Is life just a gamble?' 'Is sin a disease?' 'What is happening to hell?' In so doing he takes us through the often painful journey of conviction, repentance and conversion to a saving faith in our Lord Jesus Christ, showing how it was God himself who removed the obstacles and overcame the problems that kept us from him.

The book is divided into short, concise chapters and is written in a clear and contemporary style. The author draws from his own personal experience of salvation, highlighting the common problems of today that face us all and revealing the need for a total dependence on God in dealing with them throughout the Christian life.

> 'It is an easy book to read and I would recommend it to a new Christian seeking a greater understanding of the Christian faith'
> —*The Gospel Magazine*

EVANGELICAL PRESS, ISBN 978-085234-501-6